Frontispiece: Cathedral from SE prior to Scott's restoration.
National Monuments Record

THE BRITISH ARCHAEOLOGICAL
ASSOCIATION

CONFERENCE TRANSACTIONS
for the year 1976

II

MEDIEVAL ART AND ARCHITECTURE

at Ely Cathedral

1979

First published 1979 by Maney Publishing Ltd

Published 2017 by Routledge
2 Park Square, Milton Park, Abingdon, Oxon OX14 4RN
711 Third Avenue, New York, NY 10017, USA

Routledge is an imprint of the Taylor & Francis Group, an informa business

© The British Archaeological Association 1979

All rights reserved. No part of this book may be reprinted or reproduced or utilised in any form or by any electronic, mechanical, or other means, now known or hereafter invented, including photocopying and recording, or in any information storage or retrieval system, without permission in writing from the publishers.

Product or corporate names may be trademarks or registered trademarks, and are used only for identification and explanation without intent to infringe.

Previous volume in the series:
I. Medieval Art and Architecture at Worcester Cathedral

ISBN 13: 978-1-905981-15-1 (pbk)

CONTENTS

	PAGE
Preface	v
Observations on the Norman Plan of Ely Cathedral *by* ERIC FERNIE	1
Bishop Northwold and the Cult of St Etheldreda *by* PETER DRAPER	8
Ely Cathedral: the Fourteenth-Century Work *by* NICOLA COLDSTREAM	28
The Fourteenth-Century Tile Pavements in Prior Crauden's Chapel and in the South Transept *by* LAURENCE KEEN	47
Medieval Timberwork at Ely *by* JOHN FLETCHER	58
The Architectural History of Ely Cathedral from 1540–1840 *by* THOMAS COCKE	71
Sutton in the Isle of Ely and its Architectural Context *by* RICHARD FAWCETT	78
Short Contributions	
Denny Abbey *by* TONY BAGGS	97
Ramsey Abbey *by* TONY BAGGS	97
The Restoration of the Lady Chapel Stained Glass *by* DENNIS KING	98
Plates	at end

LIST OF ABBREVIATIONS AND SHORTENED TITLES
in use throughout the volume. See also individual contributions

Anglia Sacra	H. Wharton, *Anglia Sacra*, 2 vols (London 1691)
Archaeol. J.	*Archaeological Journal*
Atkinson	T. D. Atkinson, *An architectural history of the Benedictine Monastery of St Etheldreda at Ely* (Cambridge 1933)
B/E	N. Pevsner et al., ed., *The Buildings of England* (Harmondsworth various dates)
Bentham	J. Bentham, *The History and Antiquities of the Cathedral Church of Ely* (Cambridge 1771)
B.L.	British Library
Chapman	F. R. Chapman, *The Sacrist Rolls of Ely*, 2 vols (Cambridge 1907)
JBAA	*Journal of the British Archaeological Association*
Ladds	S. Inskipp Ladds, 'The Monastery of Ely', *Cambridgeshire and Huntingdonshire Archaeological Society*, v (1930), 41 seq., reprinted as *The Monastery of Ely* (Ely 1930)
Stewart	D. J. Stewart, *On the Architectural History of Ely Cathedral* (London 1868)
VCH	Victoria History of the Counties of England

Preface

This is the second volume in the series launched by the British Archaeological Association in which are to be published the transactions of the annual conferences devoted to the study of a major medieval monument and its surrounding area. As in the case of the first volume the unavoidable delay in publishing the transactions has meant that some of the papers are not in the form that they were delivered to the conference and that not all the papers were available for publication in the present volume. The editors have therefore taken the opportunity to include some additional plates, especially plans, which may not be referred to directly in any of the papers but which, it is felt, will make the volume a more useful contribution to the study of this remarkable building. The editors would like to thank Kit Galbraith for her assistance in providing a number of the plates for this volume and Susan Bird for the cover design. On behalf of the Association we acknowledge the generous grants received from the Pilgrim Trust and the British Academy towards the cost of publication.

NICOLA COLDSTREAM
PETER DRAPER
Hon. Editors

Observations on the Norman Plan of Ely Cathedral

By Eric Fernie

The church begun by Abbot Simeon during his period of office between 1081 and 1093 had an aisled presbytery of four bays with a stilted apse, a crossing and aisled transepts of four bays each, an aisled nave of thirteen bays with a cloister flanking eight of them on the south side, and finally a western transept possibly with a galilee porch. While the crossing, much of the presbytery and the north arm of the western transept have been lost, enough remains to permit the establishing of all the major dimensions (Fig. 1). These suggest the existence of a unit and a system of proportions which can be demonstrated most clearly in the widths of the nave and aisles.

Because the arcade walls have been inaccurately laid out at an angle to the aisle walls, the aisles are not only different in width from each other but are also of differing widths at either end. Their intended size is however retrievable from the fact that all the other transverse dimensions are relatively constant. The total internal width measured to the back of the blind arcading enlarges gently from east to west from 23.49 m to 23.61 m. The internal width of the nave has the same consistent variation, ranging from 10.06 m to 10.14 m, and the arcade walls vary in thickness only a centimetre or so on either side of 1.68 m. The intended aisle widths should therefore be what is left when the nave and the arcade walls are subtracted from the total width, that is, in bay seven for instance, 23.57 m minus 10.06, 1.68 and 1.70 m, which equals 10.13 m or two aisles of 5.06 m each. The likelihood that this is close to the intended aisle width is supported by its being half the width of the nave (Fig. 2a).

These figures are all reducible to the standard English foot of 0.3048 m giving as in Fig. 2c a total width of 77 ft, a nave of 33 ft, aisles of 16 ft 6 in and arcade walls 5 ft 6 in thick. The feet can in turn be grouped into larger units such as sixteen and a half, so that each aisle is one unit and the nave two. This unit has the attraction of being the length of the English perch, but while it may represent a starting point it suffers the disadvantage of translating the 77 ft overall width into four and two thirds units. Units of 5 ft 6 in make each aisle three units, the nave six and each arcade wall one (Fig. 2b), and since two such units equal 11 ft the relationship with 77 ft, 33 ft and 22 ft is clear.[1] A unit of this size also enables one to make sense of the other proportions of the plan. Proportional systems, like units, are not necessarily mutually exclusive, so one needs to extract the one which most satisfactorily explains the positions of the major elements in the building. The combined width of nave and aisles for instance is fourteen units of 5 ft 6 in, made up of six for the nave and four for each aisle and arcade wall, 4, 6, 4. Therefore the distance from one aisle wall to the axis of the church is 38 ft 6 in or seven units of 5 ft 6 in, to the opposite arcade wall 55 ft or ten units, and to the opposite aisle wall 77 ft or fourteen units (Fig. 2b). The pairs of numbers of feet, 38½:55, 55:77 (7:10, and 10:14 units), have the same relationship as that which the side of a square has to its diagonal, that is one to the square root of two, 1 to 1.4142. Using larger figures, this is 10 to 14.142 or in round numbers, 10 to 14. In the sequence of numerical approximations to the square root of two every second element doubles, thus 1:1.4142:2, or 10:14:20, or 12:17:24:34:48:68, or as in the present case 7:10:14. Such a proportional system may appear unlikely, but it is necessary to test both it and the 5 ft 6 in unit on the rest of the plan.

The common, not to say standard, basic proportion found in the larger Anglo-Norman churches is between a western arm equal to one and a total length to the chord of the apse equal to the square root of two. In other words the length of the church to the western wall of the transept multiplied by root two produces an extra length equal to the eastern arm consisting of the transept width and the presbytery up to the chord of the apse. The western arm at Ely measured along the north aisle between the interior of the façade and the interior of the western wall of the transept is 263 ft 6 in (80.32 m). 264 ft is the equivalent of forty-eight units of 5 ft 6 in, and forty-eight, as noted above, is part of the root two sequence 12, 17, 24, 34, 48, 68, so that 48 multiplied by root two produces an extra 20. Twenty units equal 110 ft, and the eastern arm to the centre of the chancel arch is 110 ft 10 in (33.78 m). The combined length of the two arms measured along the north aisle is 374 ft 4 in (114.10 m), in comparison with an ideal of 374 ft, so that the discrepancies can be explained by a misplacing by six or seven inches of the western wall of the transept, which seems a reasonable margin of error. That this seemingly over-complex argument is likely to be correct is suggested by two things. First, 110 is the next number in the root two sequence 38½, 55, 77, so that an eastern arm 77 ft wide by 110 ft long forms a rectangle with sides as one to root two. Second, the length of the presbytery, that is the eastern arm without the width of the transept, is 78 ft (23.78 m) suggesting it was intended to form a square with the 77 ft width. The eastern arm taken from the west side of the crossing would thus be root two where the presbytery is one, since 77 times root two equals 110. The 33 ft difference between 77 ft and 110 ft is the width of the transept, which will therefore form a square crossing with the nave. The 179 ft 5 in length of the main transept is the only major dimension not divisible into units of 5 ft 6 in, but the three sections of the south arm, the width of nave and aisles, and the north arm relate to one another in exactly the same way as do the nave and its two aisles. That is, one transept arm of 51 ft 4 in plus the 77 ft width of nave and aisles equals 128 ft 4 in and that times root two, as ten to fourteen, equals 179 ft 8 in. As for the western transept, its extant southern half is 65 ft 11 in long from the axis of the church, suggesting a total length of 131 ft 10 in or half the 263 ft 6 in length of the western arm (in round figures 66 ft, 132 ft, 264 ft). The nave excluding the western transept measures 220 ft 10 in (67.32 m) along the north aisle. 220 ft would be twice the length of the eastern arm, but the ten inch discrepancy renders the intention uncertain.

The only major feature still remaining to be explained is the side of the cloister, about 131 ft (39.92 m) along the south aisle.[2] This figure is nine inches less than

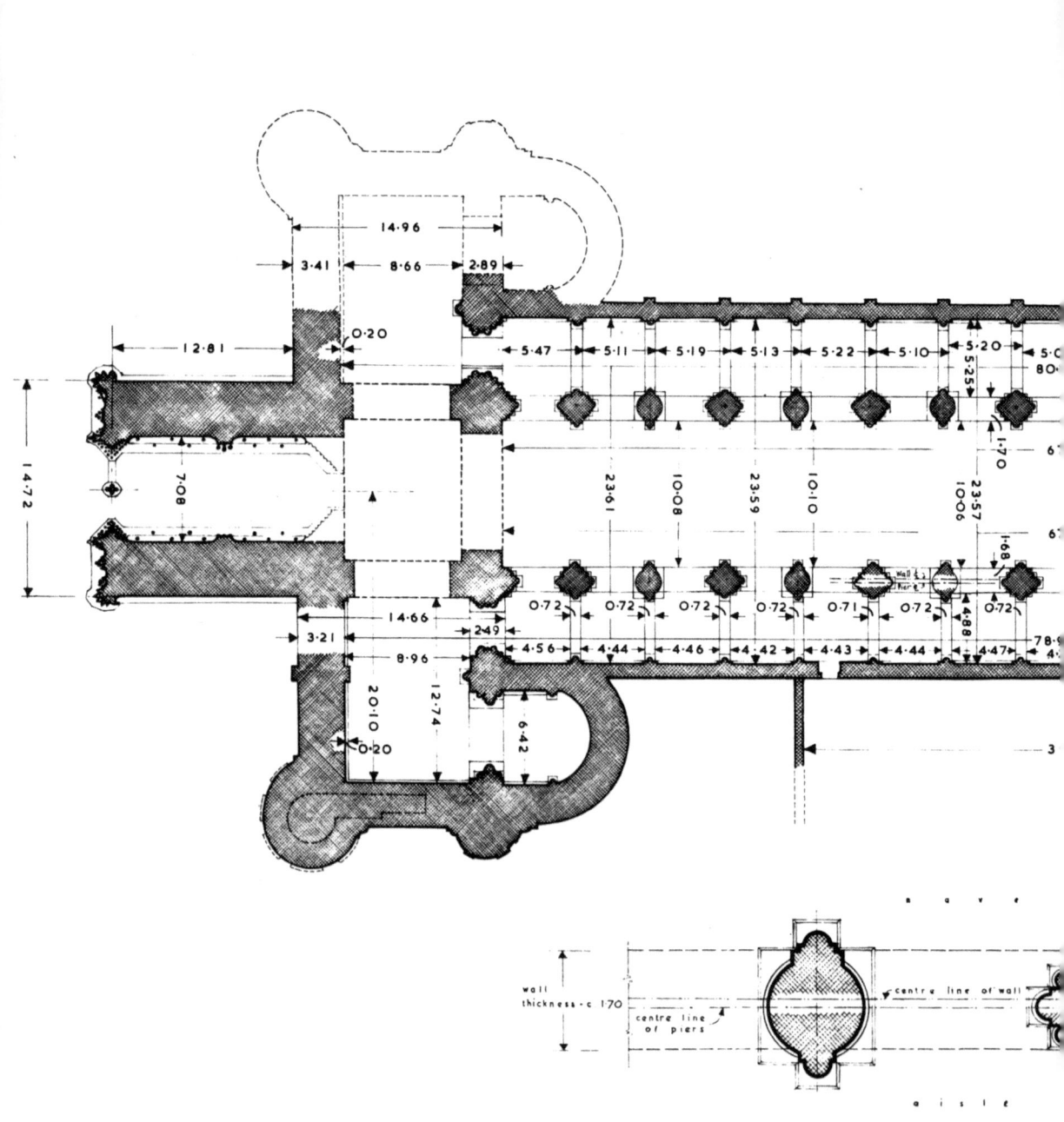

DETAIL SHEWING DISPOSITION OF TYP

SCALE OF PLAN : 1 – 200m

SCALE : 1 – 50.

FIG. 1. Plan of

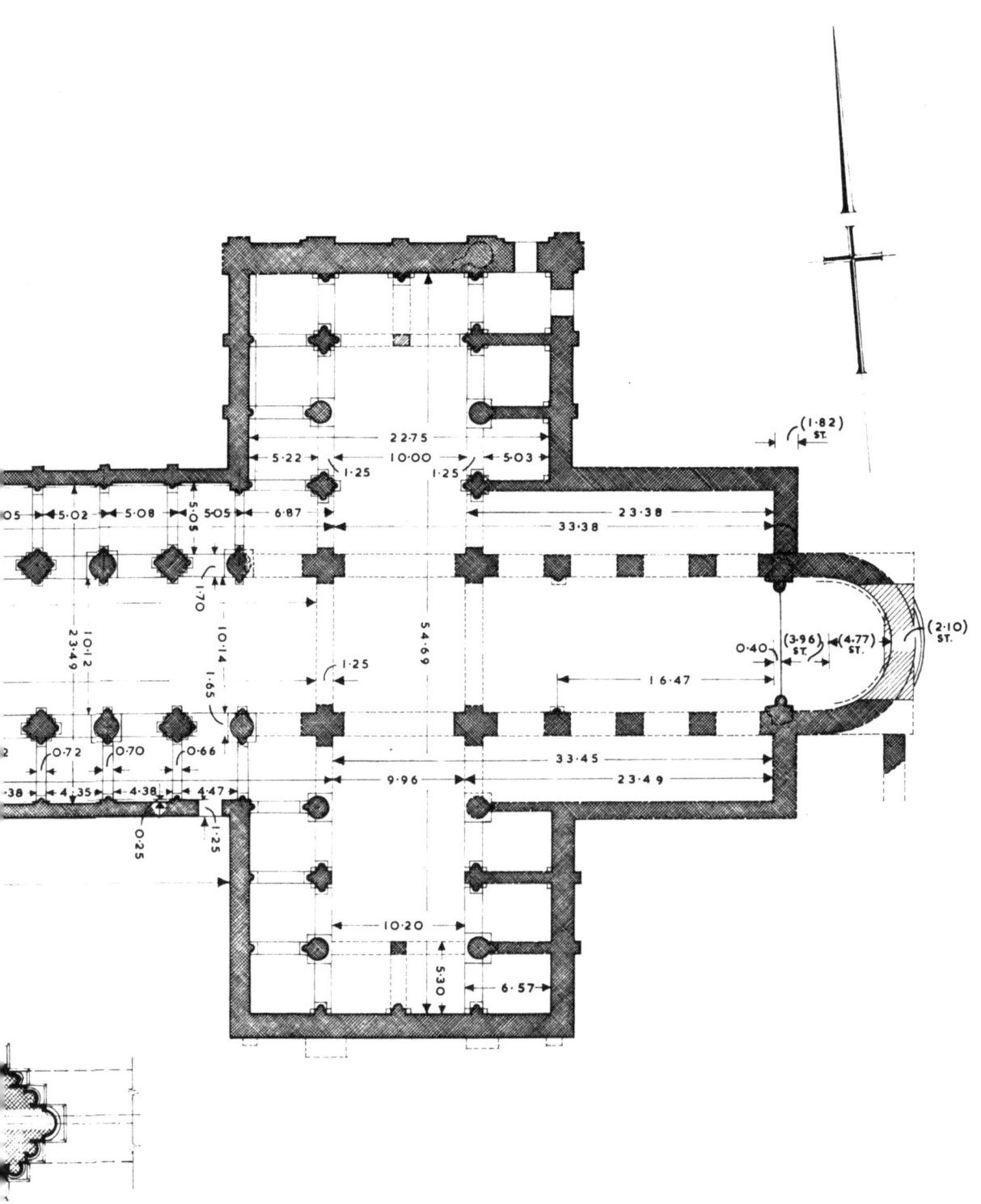

NAVE PIERS

NOTE : 'ST' INDICATES D.J. STEWART. 1868.

ECF mens et ADJ del.

rman Cathedral

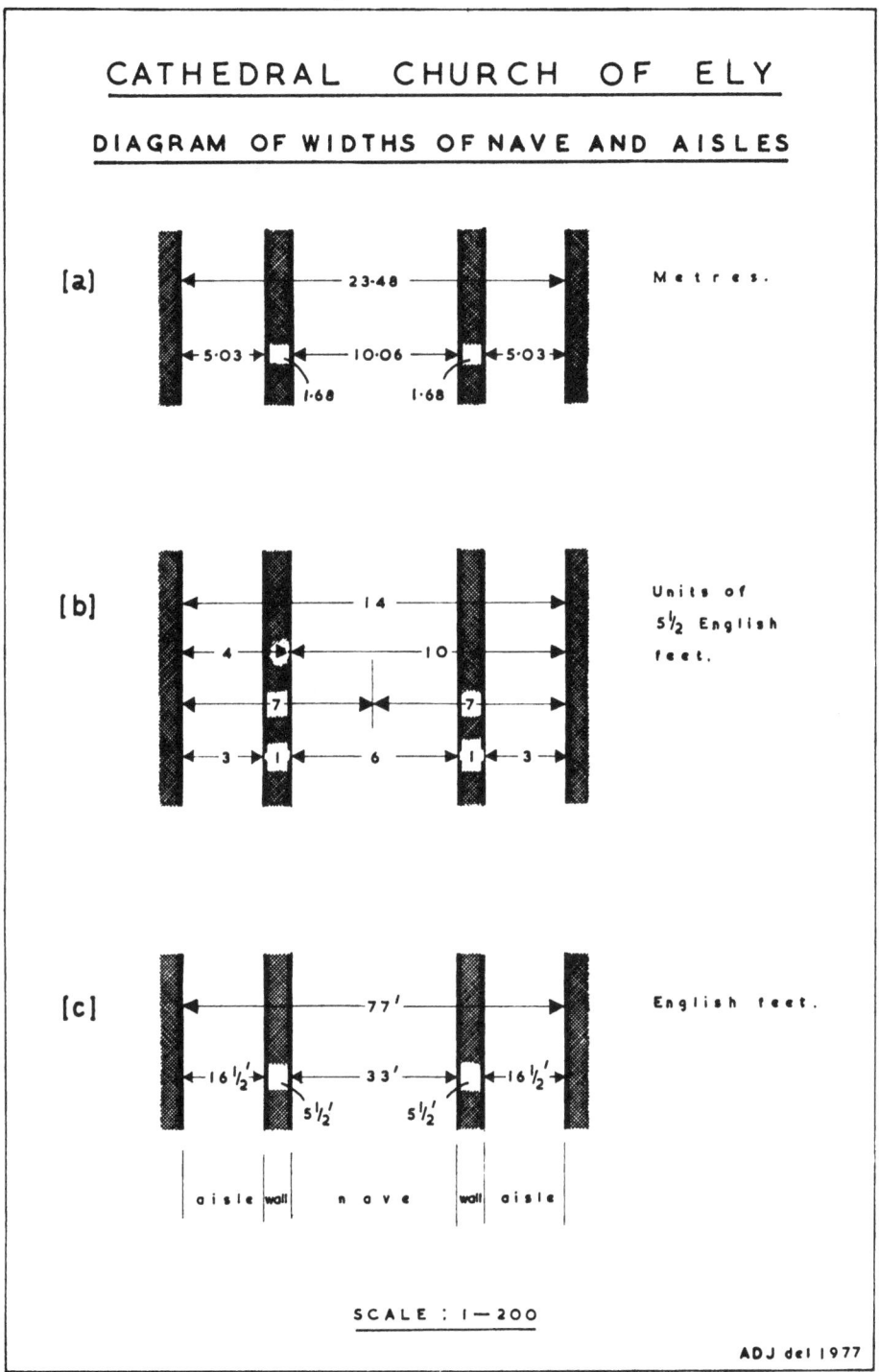

FIG. 2. Diagram of widths of nave and aisles

half the 263 ft 6 in western arm, which is again a questionable margin of error. However, the 263 ft 6 in length, like all the east–west dimensions used so far, is that along the north aisle, while the western arm measured along the south aisle is somewhat shorter at 261 ft 10 in (79.80 m), half of which is 130 ft 11 in, or the side of the cloister. In the same regard the length of the nave proper along the south aisle is 220 ft 2 in (67.10 m) which reduces the discrepancy between the actual nave length and the suggested one of 220 ft noted above to within acceptable limits. To conclude, in terms of the 5 ft 6 in unit the building can be described as follows. The nave is six units wide and the nave and aisles together fourteen; the western arm is a rectangle forty-eight by fourteen and the eastern arm twenty by fourteen, while the presbytery is a square fourteen by fourteen; the nave is forty units long and the western transept and cloister each twenty-four units. On a larger scale the cloister multiplied by two equals the western arm, which multiplied by root two produces the length of the eastern arm, and the eastern arm multiplied by two equals the nave.

The proportion one to the square root of two occurs with great regularity in the larger Anglo-Norman churches and is common at least as far back as the fourth century.[3] At St-Pauls-without-the-walls in Rome for instance the length of the nave multiplied by root two equals the total length, and the western arm is a rectangle with sides as one to root two, both features analogous to Ely. While the similarities between these two buildings can and indeed should be explained as due to the survival of a tradition, there are grounds for proposing a more specific link, namely that the great length of the more important Anglo-Norman churches is an attempt to emulate the size of the largest Early Christian basilicas in Rome. The total internal length of St Paul's is 128.38 m, of St Peter's about 120 m without the narthex and about 133 m with it. Ely is about 123 m long internally, Norwich cathedral just under 132 m, and Winchester cathedral 143 m even excluding its western element. By contrast the early 11th-century cathedral at Rouen is at most 98 m long, and William the Conqueror's major pre-Conquest monastic foundation, S. Etienne at Caen, is 75.59 m without its western towers (less than the nave of Norwich) and only 84 m with them. The total width of the nave and aisles is comparable at Rouen, Caen, Winchester, Ely and Norwich (approximating to the width of the nave alone at St Peter's and St Paul's), so the important change that takes place in the 11th century is one of length, as can be illustrated by superimposing the plans of S. Etienne and Ely on to the plan of St Paul's (Figs 3, 4).

Turning to more immediate sources, the closest in date and form is Winchester cathedral. Simeon had been prior there before coming to Ely, and the reconstruction of Winchester was begun by his brother Walkelin in 1079,[4] an unusual instance of the institutional connection actually producing the architectural results which are normally assumed to follow in such an instance, but which seldom do. The two buildings have in common an exceptional length, an aisled transept, a huge feature at the western end of the nave, a three-storey elevation, and the ubiquitous use of the square root of two.

There are however many differences, such as the lack of a crypt at Ely. This cannot have been occasioned by a desire to avoid the appalling constructional

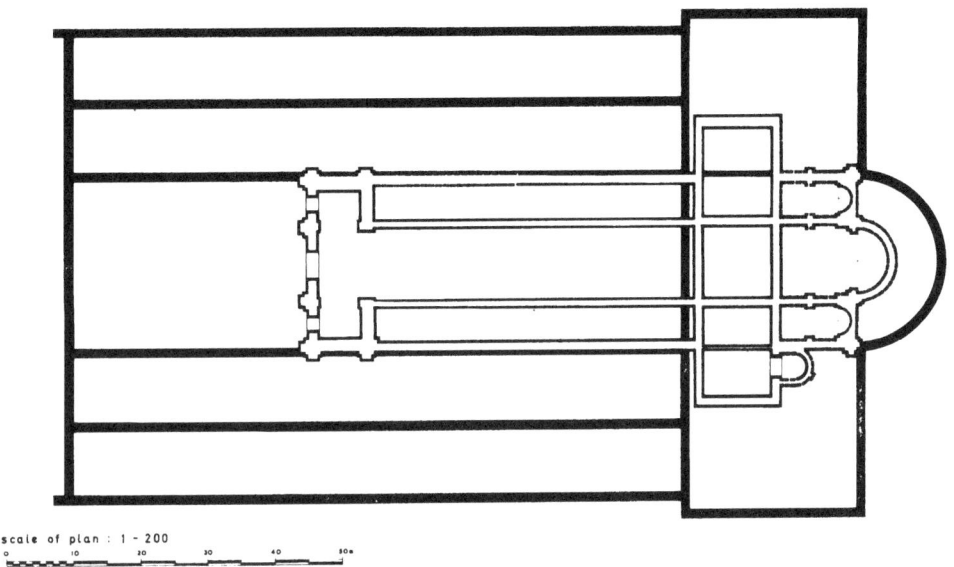

Fig. 3. Plan of S. Paolo-fuori-le-Mura, Rome with that of S. Etienne, Caen superimposed

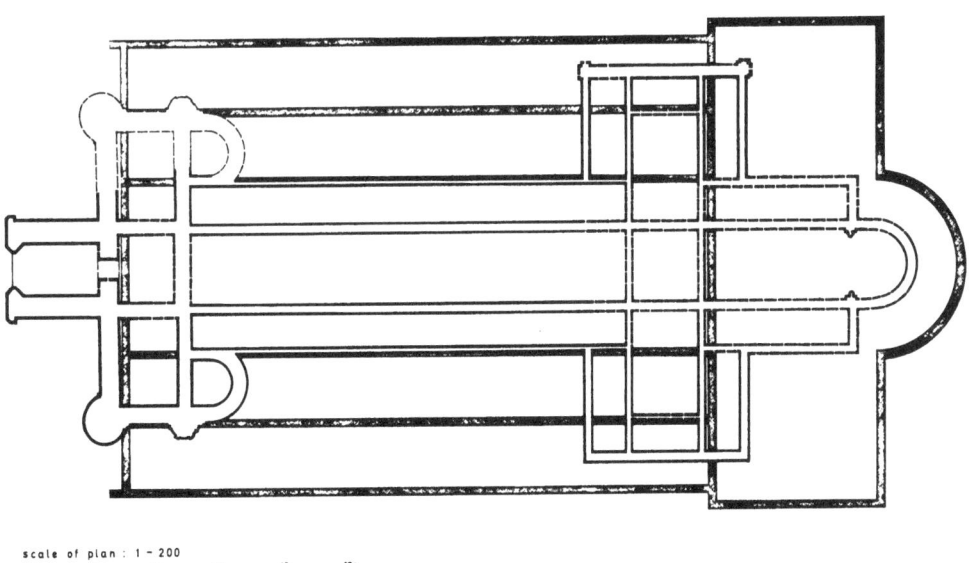

Fig. 4. Plan of S. Paolo-fuori-le-Mura, Rome with that of Ely cathedral superimposed

difficulties which must have accompanied the feature at Winchester, since Ely, despite its location in the fens, stands high on a promontory with its east end near a gentle slope, ideal for the construction of a lower storey. It may be that the crypt at Winchester was built specifically to raise the sanctuary above the water-table as a sort of liturgical damp-course.[5] Against this however one can cite Norwich cathedral which is low-lying, near a river (with a nearby parish church called St Mary in the Marsh), but without a crypt. Neither can a crypt be connected with the presence of important relics. It is true that Norwich without a crypt had no Saint of note and Winchester with one had St Swithun, but he was no more eminent than St Etheldreda or St Cuthbert. One is left with the bizarre contention that crypts occur where there are important relics and a danger of flooding, as at Winchester, St Augustine's Canterbury, and Bury St Edmunds. This may not be so wide of the mark though in the end the most likely explanation could be a desire for a raised sanctuary.

It is difficult to explain the second difference, namely the lack of an ambulatory at Ely, except by suggesting that there was as much of an ambulatory in Simeon's church as there is at the east end of Northwold's 13th-century extension. In other words the large fore-bay between chancel arch and apse could have provided some access to the shrine of St Etheldreda placed east of the high altar,[6] while the squaring off of the east end may have been intended to provide more adequate accommodation for all four shrines, perhaps with an extension of the side aisles to form an elbow ambulatory behind the high altar (probably situated one bay west of the chancel arch), as suggested by the fragments of wall at the south east extremity of the excavated section (Fig. 1).[7]

Lastly, there is no galilee at Winchester while there may have been one at Ely. For nearly two centuries there has been a debate on the incompatibility of the documentary and stylistic evidence for the date of this westernmost structure. According to the texts it was built by Bishop Eustace (1197–1215) and according to its style it has been dated to the time of Northwold's presbytery around 1240. Essex's 18th-century plan showing the church 'as it was built' gives it a galilee. He supports his inclusion of the feature by arguing that it would be necessary as a support for the western tower; that its walls are very thick, suggesting a buttressing function; that there is a huge arch opening westwards out of the crossing with no indication of a contraction; and lastly, that there are traces of older walls remaining between the Norman walls and the new galilee. No signs of this last point are now visible and it is not clear what Essex meant, but the other three observations are cogent and support the view that a western element was envisaged. Stevenson, summarising Essex, concludes that Eustace rebuilt the galilee, but this assumption is unnecessary. Bishop Ridel (1174–1189), to quote Bentham, 'carried on the new work and the tower at the west end almost to the top'. In other words it is possible that Eustace merely built the galilee in an up-to-date style as his part of the completion of the Norman design.[8] The question must however remain open both because the 5 ft 6 in unit does not occur in the galilee and because of the contradictory nature of the stylistic evidence.

REFERENCES

1. Despite this rejection of the perch I must record my indebtedness to Peter Kidson for introducing it at the conference, since the reading of the plan in feet makes its character much clearer and has enabled me to correct a number of important points. For the perch see P. Grierson, *English Linear Measures* (Reading 1972), passim. The five-and-a-half-foot unit is not a common one. J. B. Ward-Perkins, *Quarrying in Antiquity* (London 1971), p. 23, notes a standard column length of five and a half Roman feet in use at Ephesus.
2. The western wall of the cloister, that which determines its 131 ft (39.92 m) length, must have lain in line with the respond between the ninth and tenth bays of the south aisle. This does not mean that its position was determined by the bays but rather the contrary, since the latter vary a great deal in length, being close to 16 ft 7 in (5.01 m) in bays two to six and thereafter increasing to nearer 17 ft 1 in (5.20 m). The cloister length of eight bays relates to the thirteen of the nave as the two elements of the golden section as Dr Kidson pointed out, but given the absence of this proportion elsewhere in the plan there is nothing to indicate that it was intended. The significance of the variations and discrepancies noted should be evaluated as a percentage of the total measurement.
3. The basic work on the use of the proportion one to root two in classical and medieval architecture is P. Kidson, *Systems of measurement and proportion in early medieval architecture*, 2 vols (unpublished doctoral thesis, University of London, 1956). See also E. Fernie, 'The ground plan of Norwich Cathedral and the square root of two', *JBAA*, CXXIX (1976), 77–86. The most important omission from that essay is the fact that Norwich, like Ely, has an eastern arm whose length is the difference between one and root two, where the western arm is one, a proportion evident even in the numbers of bays (fourteen in the nave and six in the eastern arm composed of two for the transept width and four for the presbytery). This factor is noted at a number of points in Kidson's thesis.
4. R. Willis, 'The Architectural History of Winchester Cathedral', *Proceedings of the Archaeological Institute*, 1846 for 1845, 17–18.
5. To use Mr West's phrase.
6. E. O. Blake, ed., *Liber Eliensis*, II, Camden Society, 3rd series, 92, 1962, 144, 145.
7. Stewart, Plan, p. 25, and a discussion of the rectangular east end, p. 29.
8. Stewart, 50–52; Bentham, 143; for Essex's plan and remarks see pl. XLIX and the Addenda, 1–2; for Stevenson's remarks see the *Supplement* of 1817, 59–60.

Bishop Northwold and the Cult of Saint Etheldreda

By PETER DRAPER

Matthew Paris ends his eulogistic obituary of Bishop Hugh Northwold by describing him as 'flos Nigrorum monachorum . . . abbas abbatum . . . episcopus episcoporum'.[1] Of the many qualities that Matthew Paris admired in the only Benedictine bishop of his generation, it was Northwold's activities as an architectural patron which he singled out for particular praise. He describes the burial of Bishop Hugh 'in sua ecclesia scilicet in presbiterio nobilissimo, quod a fundamentis propriis sumptibus magnifice nimis opere indissolubili et marmareo construxerat'. Understandably, historians of the past hundred years have not endorsed Matthew Paris's high estimation of Northwold's presbytery,[2] for by the time that it was completed in 1252, the style of the building was already outdated, having none of the fashionable motifs like bar tracery being introduced at Westminster. Where reference is made to the Ely presbytery it is either as a precisely datable example of the extremely rich decoration of the mature Early English style, or as a valuable example of the 'episcopal style' which can be shown to have been financed almost entirely by the bishop.[3]

One of the reasons why Northwold's presbytery has not received the attention it deserves is, undoubtedly, that it has been overshadowed by the spectacular effects of the 14th-century work in the choir and the crossing. It should be remembered, however, that the vault of the new work was the first high vault to be built in stone at Ely, and that when first completed the extraordinarily lavish enrichment of all the architectural elements, from the piers to the vault bosses, must have formed a dramatic contrast to the simple grandeur of the Norman choir. Moreover, the original character of Northwold's work has been considerably altered, though the modifications to the fabric of the interior have been relatively minor.

These modifications began in the middle of the 14th century with the insertion of large traceried windows in the north aisle next to the 'tria altaria',[4] but the first significant alteration was made by Bishop Barnet (1366–73) in the two western bays then adjacent to the choir as rebuilt by Bishop Hotham (Pl. IX). This work involved the removal of the roof of the gallery in these two bays and the glazing of the interior gallery openings, now remodelled with flowing tracery. The aim was evidently to allow more light on to the area of the high altar and shrine. Later in the 14th century the buttressing of the presbytery was found to be unsatisfactory, so, with the exception of the two western bays, the upper parts of all the buttresses were rebuilt. The revised design involved the provision of a steeper, more effective pitch to the flying buttresses and the more judicious placing of the weight of the pinnacles. At the same time the outer wall of the gallery was heightened to permit the insertion of large traceried windows on the model of those in Bishop Hotham's choir.[5] This determination to ameliorate the unfashionable gloom of the 13th-century work led to the continuing replacement through the 15th century of the narrow lancets in the aisles by traceried windows in a similar unvarying pattern. Only the clerestory and the central part of the east wall escaped this process of modernisation.[6] The fortunate survival of the original buttresses and the external gallery wall in the two western bays enable us to reconstruct the original elevation with confidence.

More drastic than all these alterations has been the complete change in the liturgical use and arrangement of this part of the church. This started with the destruction of the shrine at the Dissolution, after which the eastern bays seem to have been used solely for burials (Pl. II), and it culminated in 1770 when James Essex moved the choir into the eastern arm with the high altar at the east end (Pl. IV). This arrangement of the choir and presbytery remains although the positions of the altar and the furnishings were altered again by George Gilbert Scott in 1848. Before turning to consider the important question of the original liturgical layout, we must first look more closely at the architectural design, and purpose, of Northwold's extension.

The fabric itself presents no great problems concerning its building history, date, or the sources of its style. It was laid out on a level and unencumbered site and, as one would expect, the main dimensions were determined by reference to those of the Norman church. This is obviously true of the width of the nave and aisles and the thickness of the aisle walls, but even the length of the new work is very close to the probable length of the former eastern arm measured to the interior of the wall of the apse (or the straight east wall which may have replaced it). The division of the new work into six bays resulted in a bay length of approximately 4.80 m. The only direct correspondence with the Norman levels in the elevation was in the clerestory passage (this was also maintained in the 14th-century choir), for the level of the gallery sill was raised about three feet in order to reduce the size of the gallery to make the proportions of the elevation conform more closely to contemporary fashion. The proportions of the main arcade, the gallery and the clerestory are thus made $3:2:2$ whereas those of the Norman elevation were $6:5:4$.[7]

Minor changes in architectural details show that the work proceeded in the usual way from east to west, with a probable pause in the work whilst the Norman apse was demolished. Slight variations between the north and south arcades indicate that the latter was constructed first. The most singular feature is the prominent use of spurs on the bases of the piers. Most of these are foliage but on the north side there are a few grotesque heads. Apart from the spurs it is immediately evident that many of the features of the design, such as the pier forms, the mouldings, the predilection for the sunk foiled motif, and the form of the vaulting corbels, derive from the recent work at Lincoln. Yet the astonishingly rich ornamentation of all the architectural elements at Ely gives it a distinct character quite unlike the comparatively austere treatment of the Lincoln nave. It is as if the architect at Ely had employed the architectural vocabulary of the Lincoln nave in the decorative spirit of St Hugh's choir. The splendour of the interior owes much to the extensive use of purbeck marble and to the way that every opportunity has been taken to exploit the sculptural quality of the thick wall (Pl. IX). But despite the fact that in the Early English style Ely presbytery is unsurpassed in the degree of surface embellishment, its importance should not be evaluated on the basis of its decorative qualities.

The real interest of the architectural design is the form that it takes in relation to the purpose for which it was designed. This aspect has been neglected in some recent literature though its importance was understood by James Bentham more than two hundred years ago. In his invaluable book he writes of Northwold's work 'This stately and sumptuous part of the fabric was first built in order to extend the church to a more convenient length for the reception of the high altar but particularly to make room for the Magnificent Shrine of S. Etheldreda and for suchlike gainful and superstitious purposes'.[8] Prejudice apart, Bentham was right in his emphasis. Indeed, this interpretation of Northwold's presbytery was made quite explicit in the 14th-century account of its miraculous preservation when the tower fell in 1322, 'illa tamen pulcra et magna fabrica eminens supra Sanctarum Virginum sepulcra, protegente Deo et meritis suae delictae virginis Etheldredae, ut speratur, ab omni laesione salvata est et fractura'.[9] The use of such elaborate architectural features and lavish surface decoration is thus explained as being wholly appropriate to the function of this part of the building.

Ely is one of a number of major churches where the eastern end was rebuilt or extended in the late 12th and early 13th century. In many cases the primary motive was to make more adequate provision for the community served by the church. There was a need, for example, to provide more altars for the increasing number proceeding to the priesthood, a process which was stimulated especially during the 13th century by the growing practice of founding chantries. In addition there seems to have been a desire to effect a clearer separation between the eastern part of the church used by the community and the general mêlée which all too often, to judge by episcopal statutes, was to be found in the nave. All the secular cathedrals and a number of the major monastic churches followed the example set by Conrad's choir at Canterbury and made the liturgical division of the church on the line of the eastern crossing piers, thus coinciding with the architectural division of the building. Of those churches that retained the choir screen west of the crossing, a few such as Norwich, Bury and Peterborough never extended their Norman choirs, and of the others which retained the position of the screen despite enlarging the east end of the church, such as Ely, Winchester, St Alban's and Westminster, the eastern extension was undertaken not to provide more space for the community but in order to make suitable provision for a major shrine.[10] This motive is made quite explicit in the Indulgence granted by Northwold in 1235 for the proposed new work at Durham 'novum opus extruere in quo ipsius sancti confessoris corpus valeat tutius pariter et honestius collocari . . .'.[11]

It is unfortunate that so little is known of the way in which major shrines were displayed in the Anglo-Norman churches for the variety of plans suggest that there was considerable variation in practice. It seems to have been common to place **the shrine** or shrines behind the high altar in the apse, but as at Ely, there was often no ambulatory to allow convenient access to the shrine.[12] The exceptionally splendid refurbishing of the shrines at S. Denis by Abbot Suger probably provided the stimulus for a renewed interest in the prominent and sumptuous display of such relics in the latter half of the 12th century. But it is at Canterbury, in the rebuilding after the fire of 1174, that we have the first certain example in England of a building where a substantial part of the east end was designed for the specific purpose of providing a spacious and splendid setting for the shrine, as at S. Denis; not as a virtually separate structure like the rotunda of St Augustine's, but as a distinct yet fully integrated 'martyrium interieur'.[13] The use of the apse and ambulatory plan for the Trinity chapel followed the usual arrangement for shrines on the Continent. It is, however, of particular interest that, although the subsequent adoption in England of the idea of making such spacious provision for a shrine undoubtedly derives from Canterbury, the only buildings to adopt the apse and ambulatory plan for this purpose were Westminster and Hailes. Significantly, both these buildings were under royal patronage. The subsequent rejection of the Canterbury solution for designing feretories is the clearest demonstration of the English determination to adopt the rectangular east end.[14]

The importance of Canterbury is not that it marks any great change in the relationship of the shrine to the high altar, but that the shrine itself was given much greater emphasis within the church and became more accessible.[15] Grabar and others[16] have shown the vital rôle played by the cult of relics in the formation and development of east ends, but the use of the rectangular form, and other idiosyncracies in the planning of churches, has caused this factor to receive much less emphasis in the discussion of English buildings.

It would be interesting to know what considerations governed Northwold's choice of the architectural form for his extension at Ely, since the topography of the site imposed no limitations. If Northwold's intention was, as I have suggested, to provide a more fashionable setting for the shrine of St Etheldreda, there were a number of possible models available by the 1230s. Apart from his former Abbey at Bury,[17] an obvious model would have been the new retrochoir of the Benedictine cathedral of Winchester. This was the first building after Canterbury where remodelling was undertaken specifically in connection with the shrine although a completely different solution was offered in the form of the rectangular hall-type outer crypt.[18] Northwold is likely to have seen Winchester but he may have felt that the junction of the new work with the Norman apse was not very satisfactory and that the setting lacked the monumental splendour to be found at Canterbury. In the interests of such grandeur he might have adopted the use of eastern transepts from Canterbury but still in conjunction with a rectangular east end as in the recent undertakings connected with important shrines at Beverley and Worcester. But, for whatever reason, Northwold turned away from the forms of east end current in the province of Canterbury and looked instead to the province of York, choosing an aisled rectangle extending full height to the east end.[19]

The origin and dissemination of this form of east end in the North is problematic.[20] The crucial building is probably the east end built by Roger de Pont l'Eveque at York. Of the many aspects of this important building which remain to be elucidated I am here concerned only whether it had a high eastern gable or whether the eastern chapels formed a low projection as at Byland. Most writers follow Willis, who preferred the latter alternative on the grounds that the east wall would have been thicker if it had had to support a high gable.[21] It is rare to fine oneself in disagreement with Willis's interpretation of archaeological evidence but there is good reason to doubt this hypothesis, because he claims that Browne shows the east wall of uniform thickness with the aisle walls. In fact this is not so. Browne shows the east wall slightly thicker than the aisle walls and equal to the dimension of the north wall of the north 'tower', but not as thick as the east and west walls of this tower.[22] Furthermore, the east wall is shown as quite five feet thick, a similar dimension to the wall of St Cross, Winchester, where, incidentally, the dimension of this wall stands in a similar relation to the aisle walls. Unfortunately, there is no trace of the vital piece of evidence, the piers of the eastern arcade, although these are postulated on all the published plans. If the existence of the two centre piers could be proved, Willis's hypothesis would be vindicated, but in the absence of such evidence there is no reason why the east wall of York should not have been full height. Moreover, the existence of such a feature at York would provide the obvious model for its appearance in Archbishop Roger's work at Ripon, where it seems likely, and for the subsequent use of this form in Cistercian, Augustinian and Benedictine churches in the North.

Nevertheless, the shrine of St William of York was not placed in Archbishop Roger's choir until 1284 and so, for Northwold, the only example of the use of this type of east end in conjunction with a major shrine was Whitby. The eastern arm of Whitby consisted of seven bays, the same number as Rievaulx which did not have an important shrine within the church. There is no evidence to indicate the form or location of St Hilda's shrine and nothing to suggest that it was of the freestanding type. It is therefore difficult to assess the possible importance of Whitby as a model for Ely.

The growing popularity of the box-like aisled rectangular east end shows that it must have proved liturgically suitable, economical to build yet offering sufficient scope for architectural design. At Ely it was also shown to be capable of providing an appropriate setting for a major shrine. In fact so suitable was it found to be that within four years of its completion Ely had served as the direct model for two of the most important eastern extensions of the 13th century; Lincoln and St Paul's. In view of this, it is obviously of some interest to try to reconstruct the original liturgical arrangment at Ely.[23]

One may begin with the fairly secure assumption that, as with Lincoln, York and other eastern extensions of this kind, the high altar remained in much the same position it had occupied in the Norman church. The reredos has left no trace on the arcade piers but it must have been removed at the Dissolution when the former choir altar was used as the high altar since Browne Willis shows the gravestone of Dean Bell (d. 1591) lying across the site it must have occupied.[24] Five bays were thus left to accommodate the feretory, the procession path and the eastern chapels. The bases of the easternmost piers are some 43 cm higher than the other piers thus establishing that there was always a step at this point though it is probable that Atkinson was right in assuming that this was originally aligned with the steps surviving in front of the chantry chapels in the aisles. This step marked the site of the eastern chapels whose altars were against the east wall.[25] The second bay would then be the procession path and the feretory contained within the remaining three bays. Browne Willis does not indicate the position of the shrine nor does he leave adequate space for it. In the most probable position he shows the tombs of Sir William Thorp and Bishop Northwold. A difficulty here is to determine what is being identified as Northwold's tomb. Browne Willis clearly shows it as a gravestone, not a tomb, and in Bentham's time Northwold's effigy was lying on top of Bishop Barnet's tomb. Nevertheless, the position indicated is the traditional position for a founder and is consistent with the description that Northwold was 'honourably buried behind the high altar at the feet of St Etheldreda in the middle of the presbytery'.[26]

The shrine itself was almost certainly of the free-standing type and fragments remaining in the church are probably to be identified as forming part of the base.[27] The style of these fragments shows them to be contemporary with the presbytery, so making Ely one of the rare instances where both the shrine and the setting were refurbished together.[28] The form of the shrine implied by these fragments would normally have an altar at the west end and this was probably situated immediately beneath the vault boss depicting St Etheldreda, which is in the centre of the fifth bay from the east (Pl. III).[29] The greater elaboration of the vaulting corbels in the two western bays would also be appropriate to their position adjacent to the high altar and the shrine.[30] It was these same two bays that were remodelled by Bishop Barnet to provide more light for this part of the church.

The location of the episcopal tombs may also be an indication of the position of the shrine. Northwold was buried at the feet of the saint and the only real question is whether he was buried within the feretory, that is, beneath the boss depicting the Coronation of the Virgin, or whether his tomb was immediately to the east of the feretory, more or less in the position indicated by Browne Willis. The tomb, or rather, heart burial of Bishop Kilkenny is probably not in its original position. In the first place it is unlikely that the present position would be described as being near to the altar of St Andrew which was probably beneath the adjacent arcade to the north of the high altar where Bishop Redman was later buried;[31] and secondly, the only case that I know in the 13th century of anyone being buried in such an honoured position in relation to a major shrine is that of Henry III. In fact, the bays on the north side were probably kept clear of tombs and would have provided the main access to the shrine for pilgrims. The Sacrist's account for 1349–50 refers to iron railings around the feretory on the north, south and east sides and to an entrance on the north. This is confirmed by an entry in the Feretrar's Rolls between 1420 and 1429 where the Feretrar's Checker, which was built out from the north aisle in the fourth bay from the east, is described as 'ex opposito hostii feretri S. Etheldr' ex parte boreali'.[32] Bishop de Luda took the position immediately to the south of the high altar[33] and Bishop Barnet was buried in the adjoining bay, which would be adjacent to the putative position for the shrine altar. The equally honoured position in the next bay to the east was later occupied by the tomb of John Tiptoft, Earl of Worcester.

It only remains to consider the position of the tomb slab of Sir William Thorp which Browne Willis shows in the centre of the feretory. Atkinson placed it in the centre of the bay immediately to the east of the high altar thereby pushing the shrine one bay further east, but there is no necessity to place the tomb in such a prominent position. The only evidence relating to the site of Thorp's tomb is that on his death he gave to the convent some plate to the value of £92 and upwards to be buried near St Audrey's shrine.[34]

Atkinson suggested that the feretory occupied three bays, Inskipp Ladds favoured two.[35] One way to decide this is to determine which bay constituted the procession path. On the exterior of the north aisle wall, third bay from the east, may still be seen the bases of jamb shafts of a former door, clearly of 13th-century date. The masonry above the bases has been carefully inserted but the wall shows signs of disturbance which make it probable that the door once existed. In the second bay the masonry is much disturbed and Browne Willis shows a door in this position with the window raised over it.[36] The date of this door is unknown. In the third bay of the south aisle there is also evidence of a blocked opening but this seems more likely to have been a cupboard, possibly for relics. It could not have provided through access for pilgrims as it leads into the monks' cemetery.[37] The remains of the door on the north side might be taken to indicate that the third bay constituted the procession path, thus leaving two bays for the eastern chapels and the shrines of SS Sexburga, Witburga and Ermenilda. At first sight the position of the tomb of Bishop Gray beneath the north arcade in the second bay would seem to corroborate this hypothesis. But, while Browne Willis describes Gray as being buried under a handsome monument, Bentham illustrates the tomb as a canopy between the two arcade piers, with short parapet walls projecting from each pier and in the gap between them a brass on the floor.[38] There is no obvious reason why Gray's tomb should have been cut through prior to 1766, the date on Bentham's plate, and it is therefore probable that the tomb was designed in this form to permit the continued use of this second bay as a procession path.

Any attempt to reconstruct the original layout at Ely is hindered by the lack of knowledge concerning the three lesser shrines. In the first place we know virtually nothing of the form of these shrines. They may have been free-standing for the statutes of Bishop Walpole contain an instruction to the monks to cease illicit conversations with women in various places including 'inter feretra sanctarum virginum'.[39] It is also recorded that Bishop Gray was responsible for decorating the head of St Sexburga with silver and gold and precious stones which might suggest a separate head reliquary.[40] The only references to the position of the shrines are in order to establish the location of the tomb of Bishop Gray and the chantry chapel of Bishop Alcock. Gray is described as being buried between two marble columns on the north side of the church 'per feretrum S. Albani et S. Ermenildae ad corneram capellae Johannes Alcock'. Atkinson initially took this to mean that the shrine of St Ermenilda (and presumably those of SS Sexburga and Witburga) was on the west side of the procession path in the third bay from the east.[41] It would, however, seem preferable to translate *per* as by, or beside, rather than between, in view of the reference to Alcock's chantry as 'iuxta tumulum S. Ermenildae'. Thus far, in three different sources, the shrines have been referred to as *feretra*, *sepulcra* and *tumuli*. This apparently indiscriminate use of terminology does nothing to clarify our problem.

A further complication arises from the position of the third figured boss on the vault. This is in the second bay, not in the centre as are the other two, but on the south side where the tiercerons meet the transverse ridge rib. The identification of this boss has caused some difficulty in the past but there seems no good reason to doubt that it represents St Peter as the attributes of the keys and the church would indicate.[42] This identification is wholly consistent with the dedication of the church in 1252 to the Virgin, St Peter and St Etheldreda. I can offer no convincing explanation for the curious position of the boss.

In view of the inconclusive nature of the archaeological and documentary evidence it is worth considering another approach to the problem; comparison with the arrangement of two east ends modelled on Ely, Lincoln and St Paul's. The addition of the Angel choir at Lincoln did not affect the position of the high altar nor of the shrine of St Hugh. This had been placed on the north side of the axial chapel and even after the translation of 1280 the shrine remained on precisely the same spot, for Browne Willis shows the site just north of the main axis.[43] In fact the Angel choir added only three bays to the east end, thus allowing one bay for the feretory. At St Paul's the entire eastern arm was rebuilt to the prodigious length of twelve bays. The choir and presbytery occupied the first seven bays east of the crossing with the reredos lying across the eighth bay. Hollar illustrates the shrine standing against the east side of the reredos with an altar facing east. This was not the original form of the shrine which was almost certainly a free-standing stone base supporting the reliquary with the altar, as usual, at the west end.[44] It was probably situated in the centre of the fourth bay from the east. The feretory thus occupied one and a half bays, with the procession path in the third bay and the two eastern bays screened off to form the Lady chapel. The space available to the east of the high altar makes St Paul's the closest parallel to Ely, and it might be used as corroborative evidence that at Ely the procession path was originally in the third bay from the east.

Such a hypothesis is in fact consistent with the archaeological evidence, for access to the procession path would then have been provided by the door in the north aisle. This door was later blocked up and a new door opened in the adjacent bay, consequent upon moving the procession path from the third to the second bay. Such a change probably involved the extension of the feretory from two bays to three and may have resulted from some reorganisation of the shrines.[45] That the procession path was in the second bay in the 15th century is demonstrated by the form of Bishop Gray's tomb and the fact that additional space could only be gained for the later chantry chapel of Bishop West by extending eastwards, demolishing the 13th-century east wall, and building a new wall between the outer faces of the buttresses.[46]

In suggesting the requirements that determined the liturgical arrangement, and thus the various functions that Northwold's presbytery was designed to fulfil, I have emphasised the significance of the shrine of St Etheldreda. It remains to ask why Northwold should have attached so much importance to the shrine of an Anglo-Saxon saint and why at this particular time? The explanation must be sought in the wider context of the renewed promotion of indigenous saints in the late 12th and 13th centuries. Despite the sceptical and even hostile attitude of the Normans to the admittedly dubious claims of some of the numerous Anglo-Saxon cults, the important saints were venerated continuously and were honourably translated into the grand new Norman churches.[47] None the less the numerous translations of Anglo-Saxon saints, or the refurbishing of their shrines,[48] in the late 12th and 13th century, does indeed suggest 'an intentional revival of the fame of those who had laid the foundations of the English church'.[49] The enhanced importance of these long-established cults is further manifested by the inclusion of the saint in the main dedication of the church, as for example, at Worcester in 1218 and Ely in 1252.[50]

It should be remembered that the sanctity of these Anglo-Saxon saints rested on 'canonisatio per viam cultus' and did not result from a formal process of Papal canonisation, a prerogative which only became firmly established during the pontificate of Innocent III.[51] In fact the first English saint to secure formal canonisation was Edward the Confessor and the successful promotion of his cult forms an important part of the context for Northwold's work at Ely. The achievement of Edward's canonisation was the result of a coincidence of interests between the king and the convent at Westminster and could be seen as a public demonstration of a relationship that the convent was carefully fostering during the 12th century. However, the use of the abbey church for coronations, and, from the time of Henry III, as the royal mausoleum, is liable to give a misleading impression of this relationship with the Angevin dynasty. William the Conqueror's political gesture in being crowned at Westminster was followed by his successors but none of them showed very much interest in the abbey, being much more concerned with their own monastic foundations. The convent was thus largely dependent on its own initiative to raise itself to a prominent position in the Benedictine hierarchy in England. A vital part of that initiative was the promotion of the cult of the Confessor. This had the advantage that it was closely connected to the other great asset of the convent, its relationship to the royal house. But Westminster was not the only abbey with such a relationship to a ruling dynasty and there can be no doubt that during the 12th century the monks at Westminster were striving to emulate the example of the community at S. Denis. The focus at S. Denis was the relics of the martyr himself but the monks, and especially Suger, were also actively encouraging the Capetian interest in their Merovingian predecessors. Despite strenuous efforts, including the forgery of documents of all kinds, the English monks were never able to match the astonishing claims made by the monks of S. Denis and accepted, in mutual self-interest, by the Capetians. But it is clear that both abbeys were trying to set themselves up as centres of national importance.[52]

There were obvious advantages to the monks of Westminster in the possession of the relics of a royal saint but the possible national significance of the canonisation of the Confessor to the Angevin dynasty, which would give the Angevins the special distinction of a saintly predecessor, also seems to have been appreciated by the Pope. Innocent II's letter deferring the application submitted by Osbert de Clare in 1138, includes the phrase 'quia cum tanta festivitas debeat fieri ad honorem et profectum totius regni ab omni regno pariter debet postulari'. It is impossible to quantify the importance to a royal house of the possession of a saintly predecessor just as it is to assess the value of the exercise of thaumaturgic powers. But that is no reason for underestimating it.[53] That benefits did accrue from such possession is clear from the efforts made by other royal houses in Europe to acquire one: Prince Waldemar of Denmark, after an unsuccessful petition in 1147, secured the canonisation of his murdered father Canute Laward in 1169; the local cult which had grown up around the Emperor Henry II at Bamberg was given formal recognition by Pope Eugenius II in 1146; and Frederick Barbarossa secured the canonisation of Charlemagne in 1166, though only from the anti-Pope Paschal III.[54]

The successful outcome of the second application for the canonisation of the Confessor in 1161 certainly owed something to the current political difficulties of Pope Alexander III, but the active participation of Henry II was a vital factor and the solemn translation of the relics was delayed until 1163 in order to ensure the presence of the king.[55] Yet after the translation, Henry seems to have shown little interest in either Westminster or the Confessor; an indifference apparently shared by his sons. John transferred his interest to St Wulfstan at Worcester but it should be remembered that his devotion was still to an Anglo-Saxon saint and to one who was intimately associated in a famous legend with the Confessor.[56] Henry III's involvement with St Edward was in many ways unexpected and his interest was really confined to the splendid shrine for his beloved patron and to the fabric of the church as a suitable setting for it. His generosity did not extend to the convent.[57]

In view of the significance to the Angevins of the solemn translation of the Confessor's relics, it must have been a bitter blow to Henry II to lose the initiative to the opposition so soon with the rapid growth of Becket's cult. This was to remain a constant embarrassment to his successors. For the significance of the cult of Becket was not just that of a martyr. In retrospect, it can be seen as the first important example of the popular veneration of a man renowned for his opposition to the king. Other examples of prominent churchmen include Bishop Grosseteste and Archbishop Edmund Rich but laymen were also honoured in this way. The best known are Simon de Montfort and Thomas of Lancaster.[58] This 'canonisation of opposition to the king', whether confirmed by formal process or resting solely on popular acclaim, was an effective device in a feudal society where saints had some precedence over kings. Opposition to the king was not the sole reason for veneration in all such cases but the topical impetus of the cults is shown by the fact that their popularity is almost invariably short-lived. This factor is of importance for the present discussion because such cults, however significant in their own day, were usually of little or no consequence as a direct stimulus to architectural enterprise. Indirectly, however, these cults may be of greater significance than has been recognised.

There can be no doubt that Henry III's ambitions for Westminster were not just an act of personal piety. They were meant to restore to St Edward, and indirectly to the Angevin dynasty, the prestige usurped by the cult of St Thomas at Canterbury. The rebuilding of Canterbury had set new standards for the setting of a major shrine and by 1240 many such shrines far surpassed the 11th-century building at Westminster in the richness and grandeur of their settings. Yet the dazzling visual splendour created by Henry III at Westminster was more than artistic rivalry; it amounted to a political statement. The veneration of Simon de Montfort was strictly forbidden in the Dictum of Kenilworth but such cults could prove very difficult to suppress. The English king did at least possess the advantage of a saintly predecessor, but even this could be a double-edged asset as John discovered.[59] For all the genuine piety of Henry III one cannot separate his personal devotion to the Confessor from this political background. The magnificent ceremony which accompanied the translation of the relics of St Edward in 1269 must have had a particularly poignant significance for Henry with the cult of Simon de Montfort then at its height.

So far the relationship between the rebuilding of Canterbury and Henry III's patronage at Westminster has been discussed without reference to what was happening elsewhere. But these seventy years, which include Northwold's presbytery at Ely, are very important for the development of English architecture. The significance of shrines in large-scale building of this period has long been recognised; less appreciated is the wide variation in the relationship between the promotion of a cult and the rebuilding associated with it.[60] A complete discussion of all the notable examples of such campaigns is beyond the scope of this paper but a few main categories can be discerned.

In earlier centuries the most obvious category included those communities which suddenly found themselves, as the result of purchase, theft, or good fortune, in possession of a popular relic. The long term popularity of the majority of cults proved to be very uncertain, but the immediate financial advantages often served to lead the community into the expensive undertaking of rebuilding their church. In England during the period under discussion the Holy Rood at Bromholm is the nearest example to this category, though Canterbury might almost be included. There the monks certainly set about the cultivation of their unexpected saintly asset in a highly professional manner. The exercise was greatly facilitated by the timely fire of 1174 which offered the opportunity to redesign the church as a fitting receptacle for the shrine, even though the vicissitudes of the relations between the monks and the archbishop, and the dispute with King John, delayed the formal translation of the relics of St Thomas to their intended location until 1220.

Although no other cult in England could match the popularity of Canterbury, its success seems to have generated in the communities of other major churches, especially cathedrals, the urgent desire, even need, to possess a notable saint. It must be emphasised that this was in addition to the innumerable miscellaneous relics that most of these buildings could boast and that the need was for the bodily remains of a major saint, preferably local, certainly indigenous. Such a saint would provide an important focus for the diocese or locality, and, at best, the promotion of the cult would result in the highly desirable combination of a sincerely pious duty with the considerable material advantage that would stem from the enhanced prestige of the church concerned. York is perhaps the classic case of the successful fulfilment of such a desire.

It was the misfortune of the canons of York that their saintly archbishops had been buried in other churches: Wilfrid at Ripon, John at Beverley and Paulinus at Rochester. Their desire to acquire the relics of a saint can be traced at least to the early 12th century with the abortive attempt to snatch the body of a former archbishop, Eata, from the church at Hexham.[61] But the need must have become very pressing with the translation of St Thomas at Canterbury and the canonisation of St Hugh of Lincoln in the same year. A successful candidate was found in William, the archbishop who had died, or been murdered, in 1154, and his admission to the calendar of saints was secured in 1226. Interestingly, his shrine remained where he had been buried, in the nave, and his relics were not translated to Roger's choir until 1284.[62] The archbishop responsible for securing the canonisation, Walter de Grey, had already supervised the beginning of a new east end at Beverley which provided a splendid new setting for the shrine of St John to rival that of St Hugh at Lincoln. In his metropolitan church, the choir was probably considered too recent to be rebuilt, so de Grey started on his grandiose transept, an undertaking that was almost certainly connected with the canonisation. Although there is no evidence, so far as I am aware, that Walter de Grey was amongst the many 13th-century bishops who were venerated as saints after death,[63] it may be significant that de Grey's tomb was probably the first episcopal tomb to have an elaborate, almost shrine-like architectural canopy.[64] The archbishop did not neglect the other great collegiate churches in the diocese. At Ripon, where, like York, the choir had been rebuilt within the last fifty years, he undertook a splendid translation of the relics of St Wilfrid in 1224.[65] The rebuilding of the east end of Southwell was not in connection with a shrine but was undertaken to enhance the prestige of the church.

Yet another category includes those instances where suitable relics were acquired and exploited in order to further a building campaign which had become necessary and had already been begun. More than a hint of opportunism on the part of the monks at Glastonbury may be discerned in the 'invention' of the relics of St Dunstan immediately following the disastrous fire of 1184. These would no doubt have afforded welcome assistance with the collection of funds for the rebuilding had not the monks of Canterbury protested so vehemently. However, the community at Glastonbury received some compensation for this setback in the acrimonious dispute with Canterbury over the possession of Dunstan's relics, with the safer discovery of the remains of Arthur and Guinevere in 1191.[66]

The extent of the damage caused by the fire of 1177 at Rochester is not known, but the monks clearly took the opportunity to undertake a substantial rebuilding of their church in the new style introduced at Canterbury. But what was the relationship between the cult of William of Perth and this new work? The relics of St Paulinus had been the greatest treasure of the monastery, but it is unlikely that his veneration was sufficiently popular by the late 12th century to attract many of the pilgrims flocking past on the road to Canterbury. The monks had become embroiled in costly litigation with Bishop Glanvill and had been forced to melt down Paulinus's shrine to pay their expenses.[67] In 1201, a baker from Perth on a pilgrimage was murdered just outside Rochester, and with the active encouragement of the monks his cult rapidly achieved considerable popularity. The cult was given formal recognition in 1256. William's sanctity seems to have been established solely on the basis of miracles effected after his death, and as the rebuilding of the east end of Rochester does not seem to have been designed to accommodate a major shrine — William's tomb was placed in the north-east transept — there are reasons for thinking that the new work had been begun in the late 12th century and that the timely murder of William was promoted as a martyrdom by the monks in connection with their building activity.[68]

It is by no means impossible that the canons of Lincoln had the intention of promoting the cult of Remigius in connection with their great rebuilding necessitated by the earthquake of 1194. In the event they were fortunate to find the desired saint in their own bishop before the work had progressed very far. The canons of Salisbury were not to be blessed with the same good fortune. The plan of the church strongly suggests that it was designed to accommodate a major shrine. Unfortunately, the first application for the canonisation of St Osmund in 1228 was unsuccessful, and though he continued to be venerated locally it was not until 1457 that he was formally canonised.[69]

It is impossible to assess accurately the financial value of these cults. Even in those few cases where records exist, the offerings at the shrine do not necessarily show the full advantage to the community. On the other hand considerable expenses could be involved as is so clearly demonstrated by the Cellarer's account for the year 1220 at Canterbury where his expenditure, mainly on hospitality, amounted to more than the offerings at the shrine.[70] The hope of immediate financial gain from relics might act as the stimulus to architectural endeavour but the ephemeral popularity of most shrines meant that few communities derived any substantial financial advantage in the long term. Perhaps the nearest analogy in our own time is with the music festivals sponsored by towns and boroughs: even when run at a loss, the sponsorship is nonetheless considered worthwhile and carries valued prestige.

The fact remains that many large-scale works were undertaken and the majority of these fall into a category which includes those churches that deliberately set about promoting the cult of a long established saint in response to the fashion set first at Westminster and then Canterbury. Although on a much less ambitious scale, the first church to emulate Canterbury by enlarging the east end in order to give greater emphasis to the shrine was Winchester. The main purpose of Bishop de Lucy's retrochoir was to improve the facilities for the display of the shrine of St Swithun. At Worcester St Wulstan had been venerated since his death but a renewed interest in his cult may be dated from 1198, more particularly from January 1201 when he began to perform a series of miracles of increasing frequency resulting in a petition to Rome for his canonisation. The Papal commission visited Worcester in 1202 and Wulstan was formally canonised in May 1203, a remarkably short time for a formal process. However, rebuilding at Worcester was not undertaken until 1224.[71] The more ambitious enterprises which follow Winchester, at Salisbury, Worcester, Beverley, and at least intended before 1229 at Durham, provide the more immediate background for Northwold's work at Ely. Whilst not minimising the subsequent influence of Henry III's work at Westminster, the chance survival of the shrine base there should not lead us to over-emphasise the significance of the form of the Confessor's shrine or its setting. The crucial building is certainly Canterbury and the survival of the fragments of the base of St Etheldreda's shrine show that Henry's enterprise was little more than an attempt to surpass the splendour of all previous examples. Canterbury was the obvious model for Westminster[72] but Henry's ideas may, conceivably, have owed something to the elaborate provision being made for the shrine of St Etheldreda, where, judging by the accounts, work was well advanced in the very years when the campaign at Westminster was being started. Ely was then the most recent of the really grand reconstructions associated directly with shrines and its internal decoration was certainly the most lavish so far. Furthermore, its importance may be judged by the fact that it provided the direct model for the two most important east ends built round shrines in the late 13th century, at Lincoln and St Paul's.[73]

Northwold's presbytery at Ely can now be appreciated as a prime example of the initiative of the bishop in the renewed promotion of the cult of an established Anglo-Saxon saint. The shrine was elevated on a fashionable free-standing base in a specially constructed feretory, and the cult was further emphasised by the inclusion of St Etheldreda in the dedication of the church. As a former Abbot of Bury, Northwold would have been well acquainted with the benefits to the monastery which accrued from the possession of a notable shrine.[74] I doubt if he would have overlooked the advantages of promoting the shrine of St Etheldreda as an essential part of an East Anglian pilgrimage route. By 1226 the fame of the miracles occurring in connection with the Rood at Bromholm had increased sufficiently to encourage Henry III to pay his first visit to that shrine. He was to make frequent pilgrimages to it between 1232 and 1248, combining it for the first time in 1234 with a visit to Walsingham which was also becoming established as a popular shrine at this time.[75] Edward I certainly included Ely in his East Anglian pilgrimage on his return to England in 1289–90.

The splendour of the ceremony of translation and dedication, attended by Henry III and the young Edward, must have been a fitting climax to the life and ambitions of Hugh Northwold. It is a sad irony that the presbytery, which should form the focus for the whole church, has been so badly served by time and historians, and its fame and attraction eclipsed by the spectacular effects of the octagon and the Lady chapel.

REFERENCES

Shortened Titles Used

Chronica Maiora: Matthew Paris, *Chronica Maiora*, ed. H. R. Luard (London, 1872–83).
COLDSTREAM (1976): Nicola Coldstream, 'English Decorated Shrine Bases', *JBAA*, CXXIX (1976), 15–34.
KEMP (1948): A. W. Kemp, *Canonisation and Authority in the Western Church* (London 1948).
SCHOLZ (1961): B. W. Scholz, 'The Canonisation of Edward the Confessor', *Speculum*, XXXVI (1961), 38–60.

1. *Chronica Maiora*, V, 454–55.
2. 'quod presbiterium nuncupatur', *Anglia Sacra*, I, 636.
3. The surviving accounts are discussed in the Appendix.
4. Chapman, II, 92.
5. The architectural alterations were analysed by Willis with his usual acumen and his observations printed in Stewart, 79–81 and plate 4. As the buttresses flanking the two western bays were not remodelled, Willis is obviously right in asserting that these alterations took place some time after the work of Bishop Barnet; cf. the careless statement in the VCH, *Cambridge and the Isle of Ely*, IV (1953), 59.
6. James Essex straightened the east wall which he reported to be two feet out of alignment (B.L. Add. MS 5842, f. 347). This operation must have been confined to the gable, the part directly affected by pressure from the wooden roof, for there are no signs of the substantial cracks or displacement of masonry lower down that would have been consequent upon a misalignment of this magnitude; cf. the account in VCH, *Cambridge and the Isle of Ely*, IV (1953), 60.
7. Ibid., 56. The proportions of the new choir at Rievaulx are 9:4:6.
8. Bentham, 285.
9. *Anglia Sacra*, I, 644.
10. The prodigious length of the eastern arm that sometimes resulted from these eastward extensions is a distinctively English characteristic. The closest parallel in France is Laon where the eastern arm was lengthened after 1205, not in connection with a shrine but to accommodate the community east of the crossing; in Germany in the 14th century a number of choirs were rebuilt as shrine chapels on the model of the Sainte Chapelle, e.g. Aachen, St Sebaldus, Nuremburg.
11. *The Rites of Durham* (Surtees Society, CVII), 149–50.
12. For the arrangement of the shrines in the Norman church at Ely see *Liber Eliensis*, ed. E. O. Blake (Camden Society 3rd Series, XCII), 228.
13. The apposite description by A. Grabar, *Martyrium. Recherches sur le culte des reliques et l'art chretien antique* (College de France 1943).
14. Strictly, *feretrum* means the shrine itself. Feretory is here used to denote that part of the building in which the shrines are displayed. For the rectangular east end see M. F. Hearn, 'The Rectangular Ambulatory in English Medieval Architecture', *Journal of the Society of Architectural Historians*, XXX, No. 3 (1971), 187–209.
15. For a recent discussion of this theme see Coldstream (1976).
16. A. Grabar, *Martyrium*, passim; R. Wallrath. 'Zur Bedeutung der mittelalterlichen Krypta', *Beitrage zur Kunst des Mittelalters*, Vortrage zum Schloss Bruhl (Berlin 1948), 54–69.
17. With an original eastern arm of five bays no extension was considered necessary at Bury. For the layout of the shrines there see M. R. James, 'On the Abbey of S. Edmund at Bury', *Cambridge Antiquarian Society* (1895), 115 seq.
18. P. Draper, 'The Retrochoir of Winchester Cathedral', *Architectural History*, Vol. 21 (1978), 1–17.
19. It is true that this form does occur in the south at St Cross, Winchester, and in collegiate churches like New Shoreham, but these are not major buildings nor did they have important shrines so are unlikely to have provided the model for Ely. That a previous bishop, John (1219–25), came from Fountains is probably not significant but an east coast connection

between East Anglia and Yorkshire would not be unexpected. There is evidence of Northwold's interest in Durham where he is known to have deposited money (*Chronica Maiora*, v, 507–8), and his Indulgence contains the fullest explanation of the purpose of the new work there, projected by Bishop Poore before 1229 but not commenced until 1242.
20. M. F. Hearn, 'The Rectangular Ambulatory . . .', *Journal of the Society of Architectural Historians* (1971), 204; P. Fergusson, 'The South Transept Elevation of Byland Abbey', *JBAA*, 3rd series, xxxviii (1975), 173.
21. R. Willis, *The Architectural History of York Cathedral* (London 1848), 11.
22. J. Browne, *The History of the Metropolitan Church of S. Peter at York* (London 1847), ii, pl. xii.
23. Much of what follows is based on earlier writers especially Atkinson though my interpretation differs.
24. Browne Willis, *A Survey of the Cathedrals of England and Wales* (London 1742), iii, 332 seq.
25. The northern altar contained the disputed relics of St Alban (for a summary of the dispute with St Alban's see R. Vaughan, *Matthew Paris* (Cambridge 1958), 198–204, and E. O. Blake, *Liber Eliensis*, Introduction, xxxviii). The southern altar was known as the altar of the relics. The dedication of the centre altar is not known. The Lady chapel remained until the 14th century in the south choir aisle.
26. *Anglia Sacra*, i, 636.
27. A hypothetical reconstruction of the shrine base is in VCH, *Cambridge and the Isle of Ely*, iv (1953), 71.
28. Coldstream (1976), 17; the shrine itself had already been refurbished and embellished by Bishop Ridel and Bishop Geoffrey de Burgh, *Anglia Sacra*, i, 635.
29. The position of this and the adjacent boss to the east depicting the Coronation of the Virgin were inadvertently transposed in the plan in the VCH (Pl. III).
30. The greater elaboration may be explained as stylistic development as these are the latest corbels.
31. *Anglia Sacra*, i, 636.
32. Atkinson, 32.
33. It is generally assumed that the original form of Bishop de Luda's tomb was modelled on that of Edmund Crouchback in Westminster Abbey and that it was subsequently 'cruelly disfigured' and the effigy destroyed in order to provide an entrance to the choir. The assumption raises two questions that have never been answered or even asked: when and why was this done? Bentham's plate, made in the late 1760s, shows the tomb in its present state with the indent of a brass serving as a step (Pl. XVIIA). So does Browne Willis's Plan of 1741 (Pl. II). As the position of the high altar was not altered there is no reason why the tomb should have been cut through prior to the Reformation. However, it is not clear why a passage should have been needed in this bay after the Dissolution when the choir altar was used as the high altar. The archaeological evidence is confined to the south side of the tomb as the north side was extensively restored and painted in the 19th century. There is slight evidence of repair visible on the buttresses and the inner shafts flanking the opening but considerable care has been taken to provide any new mouldings with the correct profile and any major disruption has been restored skilfully. Is such care likely between 1540 and the mid-18th century when no attempt seems to have been made to preserve the presumed effigy? The possibility must be entertained, however unlikely it may seem, that the tomb was constructed in its present form. The problem remains to suggest what liturgical purpose would have been served by a passage immediately to the south of the high altar. The tomb is described as 'iuxta magnum altare ad introitum veteris Capellae B. Mariae' but normal access to the Lady chapel was along the south aisle and it is hard to see why those officiating in the presbytery should have needed such direct access. Could it be that the unusual form of Bishop de Gray's monument in the fifteenth century had a precedent at Ely in the singular form of de Luda's tomb?
34. Browne Willis, *A Survey of the Cathedrals . . .*, iii, 351; VCH, *Cambridge and the Isle of Ely*, iv (1953), 70, n. 20.

35. Atkinson, plan IV and his revised plan in VCH, *Cambridge and the Isle of Ely*, IV (1953), 66; Inskipp Ladds (1930), 41 seq.
36. Browne Willis, III, plate opposite p. 330.
37. Cf. Inskipp Ladds (1930), 51–52.
38. Browne Willis, III, 355; Bentham, pl. XX.
39. *Ely Visitation Records*, ed., S. J. A. Evans, Camden Miscellany, XVII, 13.
40. *Anglia Sacra*, I, 673.
41. Atkinson later revised this arrangement for the plan in the VCH (Pl. III).
42. Inskipp Ladds (1930), 51; Atkinson, 32; C. J. P. Cave, 'Roof Bosses in Ely Cathedral', *Proceedings of the Cambridge Antiquarian Society*, XXXII (1930–31), 33–46. The apparently unusual iconography showing St Peter in a monk's cowl is an Anglo-Saxon tradition as was pointed out to me at the conference.
43. Browne Willis, III, 1. For the location of the shrine see T. J. Willson, 'The Tomb of St. Hugh at Lincoln', *Archaeol. J.*, LI, 104; Canon R. E. G. Cole and J. O. Johnston, 'The Body of St. Hugh', *Associated Architectural Societies Reports and Papers*, XXXVI (1921–22), 47–72.
44. Coldstream (1976), 24. The promotion of the cult of St Erkenwald was no doubt stimulated by the refurbishing of the shrine of St Edward at Westminster just as it had been a century before with the Confessor's canonisation, see Scholz (1961), 41.
45. It is possible that it was part of a move to make the feretory more secure following the theft in 1386, or perhaps to accommodate the tomb of Sir William Thorp. In 1455 Bishop Gray provided a new *coopertorium*.
46. Atkinson, 34, suggests that the curious door on the south side of Alcock's chantry was necessary in order to preserve the procession path blocked by Bishop Gray's monument. The manifest inconvenience of such an arrangement precludes this possibility.
47. David Knowles, *The Monastic Order in England 943–1216* (Cambridge 1941), 118–19; Scholz (1961), 38, n. 3.
48. Examples include St Frideswide in 1180, SS Felix, Ethelred and Ethelbert at Ramsey in 1192, St John at Beverley in 1193, St Oswin at Tynemouth at about the same time, St Guthlac at Croyland in 1175 and 1195 and St Edmund at Bury in 1198.
49. P. Brieger, *English Art 1216–1307*, Oxford History of English Art, Vol. 4 (Oxford 1957), 7. The interest extended beyond Anglo-Saxon saints to include the 'invention' in 1178 of the relics of St Amphibalus, the fictitious companion (or cloak?) of St Alban. The shrine was erected in 1186.
50. For Worcester, *Annales Monastici*, ed. H. R. Luard (Rolls Series), IV, 407; for Ely, *Anglia Sacra*, I, 636.
51. C. R. Cheney, *Innocent III and England* (Stuttgart 1976), Part II, Chapter I. Cf. Kemp (1948) who emphasises the importance of Alexander III.
52. R. Branner, 'Westminster Abbey and the French Court Style', *Journal of the Society of Architectural Historians*, XXIII (1964), 15; for the claims and successes at S. Denis, Gabrielle M. Spiegel, 'The Cult of S. Denis and Capetian Kingship', *Journal of Medieval History*, I (1975), 43–69, and for clear evidence of emulation by Westminster in the forging of Charters. A. S. Napier and W. H. Stevenson, *The Crawford Collection of Early Charters and Documents*, Anecdota Oxoniensia, Medieval and Modern Series, VII (Oxford 1895), 89–90.
53. Henry I seems to have been the first English king to touch for the King's Evil and it was probably during his reign that the tradition arose attributing these powers to Edward the Confessor. The political advantages for the exercise of royal government are discussed by M. Bloch, *Les Rois Thaumaturges* (Paris 1961); further exploration of some aspects and review of recent literature in Janet Nelson, 'Royal Saints and Early Medieval Kingship', *Studies in Church History*, ed. D. Baker, X (1973), 39–44. For the implications of Innocent's letter, Scholz (1961), 47, and Kemp (1948), 78.
54. Kemp (1948), 86; the role of Henry the Lion in the promotion of the cult of the Emperor Henry II is discussed by P. Lasko, *Ars Sacra*, 800–1200 (Harmondsworth 1972), 200 and 204–5; ibid., 243 and 253 for the part played by Frederick Barbarossa in the creation of the splendid shrines for the relics of Charlemagne at Aachen and the Three Magi at Cologne.

Frederick's petition for the canonisation of Charlemagne may have been prompted by Henry II, see Scholz (1961), 53, n. 71.
55. Scholz (1961), 57; Kemp (1948), 76 seq.
56. For this Angevin interest in saintly predecessors it is significant that immediately after his coronation King John visited the shrine of St Edmund at Bury. His subsequent devotion to St Wulstan may be connected with Wulstan's legendary devotion to Edward the Confessor, discussed by R. R. Darlington in the introduction to the *Vita Wulstani*, Camden Series, XI. (1928).
57. Dom Hugh Aveling, 'Westminster Abbey — The Beginnings to 1474', in *A House of Kings*, ed. E. Carpenter (London 1966), esp. 39–42.
58. J. C. Russell, 'The Canonisation of Opposition to the King in Angevin England', *Anniversary Essays in Medieval History by students of J. C. Haskins* (1929); J. W. McKenna, 'Popular Canonisation as Political Propaganda: The Cult of Archbishop Scrope', *Speculum*, XLV (1970), 608–23. According to Matthew Paris (*Chronica Maiora*, V, 330) Northwold himself spoke in these terms in reply to overtures by the King at the Parlement of 1252, 'Domine . . . ad memoriam si placet revocandum est, qualiter sancti multi pro sanctae ecclesiae libertate feliciter exularunt et gloriose occubuerunt interempti. Quid beatum Thomum commemorem martirem gloriosum? Quid beatum successorem suum beatum Edmundum nobis contemporaneum?'
59. His maltreatment of the Church was compared to the supposedly virtuous practices of the Confessor in what purports to be the text of an argument between John and the Papal nuncio Pandulf related most fully in the Burton Annals (*Annales Monastici*, I, esp. 211–13) and discussed by M. Powicke, *Stephen Langton* (Oxford 1928), 85–88.
60. I am much indebted to the excellent essay by C. R. Cheney, 'Church-building in the Middle Ages', *Bulletin of the John Rylands Library*, XXIV (1951–52), 20–36, reprinted in C. R. Cheney, *Medieval Texts and Studies* (Oxford 1973). A useful recent discussion of pilgrimages and cults in a wider context, together with an extensive bibliography, may be found in J. Sumption, *Pilgrimage: an Image of Medieval Religion* (London 1975).
61. Ailred of Rievaulx, *De Sanctis Ecclesiae Haugustaldensis*, in *Priory of Hexham*, ed. J. Raine (Surtees Society, XLIV), 1864, 202.
62. The translation at York was at the entire charge of Thomas Bek who was consecrated bishop of Durham that same day. This was clearly in emulation of his brother Anthony Bek who had paid for the translation of St Hugh at Lincoln in 1280 and immediately after that ceremony had been consecrated bishop of St David's. For the shrine at York, Coldstream (1976), 22.
63. Those officially canonised were St Hugh of Lincoln, St Edmund Rich, St Richard of Chichester and St Thomas Cantilupe. Popular veneration was accorded to several more including Bishop Grosseteste at Lincoln whose canonisation was reported in the Tewkesbury Annals for 1257 (*Annales Monastici*, I, 336), Roger Niger at St Paul's to whom Northwold referred in an Indulgence granted in 1252 as 'Beatus episcopus et Confessor', Walter Suffield at Norwich and William Bytton at Wells.
64. P. Brieger, *English Art 1216–1307* (1957), 101.
65. *Memorials of Ripon* (Surtees Society, LXXIV), I, 50.
66. C. R. Cheney, 'Church-building in the Middle Ages', *Bulletin of the John Rylands Library*, XXIV, 30.
67. Dugdale, *Monasticon Anglicanum*, ed. J. Caley (London 1817), I, 156.
68. W. St John Hope, *The Architectural History of the Cathedral Church and Monastery of S. Andrew at Rochester* (London 1900), 40, favoured the view that the monks began the eastern reconstruction encouraged by the offerings at William's shrine. For William of Perth, J. S. Richardson, 'St William of Perth and his Memorials in England', *Transactions of the Scottish Ecclesiological Society*, II, pt 1 (1906–7), 123.
69. A. R. Malden, *The Canonisation of S. Osmund*, Wiltshire Record Society (Salisbury 1901); I have discussed the liturgical arrangement in 'The Retrochoir of Winchester Cathedral', *Architectural History*, Vol. 21, 9–10.
70. C. R. Woodruff, 'Financial Aspects of the Cult of S. Thomas', *Archaeological Cantiana*, XLIV

(1932), 13–22. The offerings at Canterbury were exceptional, averaging £476 p.a. between 1198 and 1213. The records at Ely are scanty but in the fifteen extant sacrist's rolls between 1322 and 1360 the maximum amount received at the shrine was £40 2/- out of a total income entered by the sacrist of £211 6/2 (Chapman, I, 119, Appendix A).
71. C. R. Cheney, *Innocent III and England* (Stuttgart 1976), 56–58; B. Singleton, 'The Remodelling of the East End of Worcester Cathedral in the Earlier Part of the Thirteenth Century', *Medieval Art and Architecture at Worcester Cathedral*, The British Archaeological Association Conference Transactions for 1975 (London 1978), 105–15.
72. Coldstream (1976), 26–27; L. E. Tanner, 'Some representations of St Edward the Confessor . . .', *JBAA*, 3rd series, XVI (1953), 4.
73. The canons of St Paul's no doubt deliberately chose a different plan to that of Westminster Abbey, see note 44 above.
74. For details of Northwold's biography and his building activity at Bury, *The Chronicle of the Election of Hugh, Abbot of Bury S. Edmund's and later Bishop of Ely*, ed. R. M. Thompson (Oxford 1974), Appendix v.
75. J. C. Dickinson, *The Shrine of Our Lady of Walsingham* (Cambridge 1956); F. Wormald, 'The Rood of Bromholm', *Journal of the Warburg and Courtauld Institutes*, I (1937–38), 31–45.

APPENDIX I

In the Cottonian manuscript Tiberius B ii in the British Library there exists a set of accounts relating to Northwold's work at Ely. The accounts appear in the context of various memoranda prepared for the bishop and his immediate predecessors. The sources of income are carefully itemised but only the total is given for the annual expenditure. It is clear, therefore, that these are not the working accounts which would be primarily concerned with recording the disbursements to craftsmen and suppliers. Such records would doubtless have been kept by the Sacrist.

The surviving accounts which begin in 1240 are rendered initially by the Sacrist together with *socius suus* Richard de Stradebroc. After the first four years Richard alone renders the account until 1246–47 when he is succeeded by Adam de Burgo. The sources of income include contributions from the convent and its officers but overall the bishop is shown to have contributed more than three-quarters of the funds. The accounts really take the form of financial memoranda recording this fact. This interpretation is supported by the notes made under the years 1239–40 and 1244–45 when the expenditure exceeded the income for those years, in which the clerk notes that the deficit is owed to the Sacrist by the bishop. It is probable that the accounts are not complete for they record only half the expenditure mentioned by the chronicle sources.

The first account, for the year 1239–40, is described as 'anno vij ab incepcione nove fabrice ecclesie de Ely' (Table I). This provides a starting date of 1234. Beneath this first entry is a list of the annual receipts for the first six years. Stewart was led to misinterpret this list because three of the sums coincide precisely with figures given in the accounts for later years. The fourth and fifth receipts correspond to the income for the years 1239–40 and 1240–42 and the sixth receipt is the same as the expenditure recorded for 1242–43. Stewart thus assumed that the sums did in fact refer to those years and redistributed the first three receipts to cover the years 1234–39. This he was able to do by postulating that the three sums listed for the second receipt and the two for the third receipt should be understood as referring to separate years. Unfortunately, he then had to provide a rather forced explanation for the negligible sums collected in these early years. In addition, he had to suppose that the Sacrist and the clerk had inadvertently inverted the figures for income and expenditure in the account for 1242–43. That this is not the case can be proved by the note at the end of the account which records that the clerks are owed £21. 17s. 6d., the amount overspent. Furthermore, following the account for 1245–46 three sums are recorded. The first is the total income for the preceding six years (1240–46). The second gives the total for the first six receipts and the third shows the grand total of the income received to date. There can therefore be no doubt that the list of receipts does record the income for the first six years despite the coincidences which misled Stewart. No expenditure is recorded for these years but in view of the nature of these accounts this cannot be construed as an indication that work had not yet begun.

At face value the accounts suggest an exceptionally well ordered campaign with a meticulous balance being maintained between expenditure and income. Indeed for the years 1245–46 and 1247–48 the two figures are identical and the same is nearly true of the two succeeding years. The obvious explanation is that the income was made up, doubtless by the bishop, to meet a known level of expenditure. The alternative explanation, that the total expenditure was entered to account for the disbursement of the funds, is perhaps uncharitable. That the former explanation is correct is indicated by the sudden doubling of the income to meet a similar rise in the expenditure in 1246. The exceptional outlay during the years 1246–49 presumably results from a period of intense activity in the building campaign. In other respects these accounts provide no guide to the progress of the work.

Even as a record of the financing of the presbytery these accounts must be used with caution. But they do provide firm evidence for dating the work and they do corroborate Matthew Paris's assertion that Northwold built the presbytery '*sumptibus suis*'.

TABLE I

British Library Add. MSS Tiberius B ii, f. 246–48
The first entry, for the year 1239–40 is described 'anno vij ab incepcione nove fabrice ecclesie de Ely'. Beneath this entry is listed:

Prima recepta ad novam fabricam . . .	£276 9/3
Secunda recepta	£109 19/3; £39 8/–; 10 marcs (£6 13/4)
Tertia ,,	£200 4/10; £2 1/3
Quarta ,,	£182 13/6
Quinta ,,	£202 5/9
Sexta ,,	£113 15/2
Total	£1,135 19/7

Year of Account	Receipts	Bishop's Contribution	Expenditure	Balance to be carried forward	Deficit owed by the Bishop
1239–40	£182 13/6	£138	£156 18/9	£28 14/8	
1240–42	£202 5/9	£140 13/4	£184 7/6	£17 18/3	
1242–43	£ 91 17/8	£ 54 6/8	£113 15/2		£21 17/6
1243–44	£204 5/3	£168 13/4	£188 1/8	£16 3/7	
1244–45	£166 17/9	£108 19/10	£201 –/5		£34 2/8
1245–46	£192 19/–		£192 19/–		
1246–47	£476 16/2	£445 5/2	£452 10/6	£24 5/8	
1247–48	£322 13/3	£269 12/11	£322 13/3		
1248–49	£373 1/5	£343 13/9	£373 13/–		11/6
1249–50	£207 8/2	£180 14/4	£209 1/3		£ 1 13/1
1250	£ 26 3/10		£ 49 9/11		£23 6/–

N.B. The figures are transcribed as written, disregarding fractions of a penny which are often scarcely legible. No attempt has been made to correct the figures to ensure mathematical consistency as Stewart did in his table (D. J. Stewart, 71).

Ely Cathedral: the Fourteenth-Century Work

By NICOLA COLDSTREAM

The building programme at Ely in the second quarter of the 14th century included, in the octagon and Lady chapel, two of the most spectacular buildings of a notably splendid period in English architecture.[1] In addition the surviving Sacrist Rolls give abundant documentary evidence of the building campaign, of a kind rarely found outside the records of the King's works. Yet for some years Ely has received little attention as an architectural undertaking in its own right, although some attempt has been made to place it in the Decorated style as a whole. Despite their stylistic merits and the written evidence, the buildings remain a puzzle, both as to exact dating and the sources of their styles. It is the purpose of this paper to offer solutions to some of these problems.

The written sources establish limits of dating within which it is possible to argue. Chapman's introduction to the Sacrist Rolls[2] includes a thorough discussion of the chronology of the octagon and choir bays, and his conclusions remain acceptable. The octagon was built from 1322–28 after the fall of the Norman central tower in 1322,[3] and the wooden lantern above was done in stages, the lower vault being up by 1334, the upper boss painted in 1339–40.[4] The bell-makers were at work in 1341.[5] The choir bays, said to have been finished by the death of bishop Hotham in 1336, were probably finished in 1337 when the vault may have been painted.[6] The ritual choir was fitted and furnished in 1341–42, by which time Hotham's tomb was completed.[7] After 1337 the work in the choir and octagon consisted of finishing touches and repairs, and we may conclude that the masons were free of the main structure by 1337.

The sacrist was concerned only with the *novum opus*, the octagon and the ritual choir. He appears to have been involved to some extent with the building of the new choir bays: although *Anglia Sacra* records that Hotham paid for them, one of the few certain references to the building of the bays is in the Sacrist Roll for 1323–24, where payment is made in two separate entries for sharpening the axes of the sacrist's men and the bishop's men.[8] If Chapman is right in thinking that the vault referred to in 1337 is that of the choir,[9] the sacrist must have taken responsibility for finishing the bays after the bishop's death, and the reference to the axe-sharpening suggests that he supervised early work in the choir. In view of the similarities between choir and octagon, the distinction of the groups may not be important.

Reference to the Lady chapel in the Sacrist Rolls is purely incidental. It was founded in 1321, before the central tower fell. Work was going ahead in 1322–23,[10] and it must have been structurally almost complete when Bishop Montacute was buried before the high altar in 1345.[11] It was probably consecrated in 1353, with the east and west windows still to be finished.[12] These dates are complemented by the chronicler's assertion that the chapel was built in the lifetime of John of Wisbech, the monk in charge, who died in 1349.[13] The remaining major building of the group, Prior Crauden's chapel, is dated by the Treasurer's Roll of 1324–25, which recorded the payment of more than £138 towards the prior's chapel, a sum large enough to be regarded by Pevsner as a final payment.[14] Thus the Lady chapel was probably the first building on the site to be started, but the last to be finished.

A large workforce was kept busy at Ely for about twenty-five years, and the works in the cathedral were only part of its activities. The prior's chapel was in a set of new rooms erected at the same time as two large halls for monks and guests. The sacrist built many offices and workshops about the precinct. John Crauden is said to have rescued the monastery from considerable debt,[15] but insolvency was no deterrent to splendour. The financial responsibility for the different buildings lay with different people. The *novum opus* was funded partly by a subscription list throughout the diocese, and partly by the monks' sacrifice of special wine, money and sweet things until the work should be done.[16] As we have seen, Hotham is supposed to have paid for the choir bays, and some money came from the fund for the *novum opus*. Crauden and Montacute were said to have contributed to the building of the Lady chapel, and John of Wisbech is alleged to have found a pot of bronze coins in the foundations, which he guarded jealously and used for the building fund.[17]

Most authorities see Norwich and Lincolnshire as the sources of the Decorated work at Ely, Harvey claiming the presence of John Ramsey of Norwich as architect.[18] Bock prefers a London connection, a view also supported by Harvey, who speculated that 'cuidam de Londonia', who set out the octagon, was William Hurley, the King's master carpenter.[19] The more architectural, less decorated, parts of the work — the octagon, choir bays and Prior Crauden's chapel — are ascribed to Norwich masons, and the highly decorated Lady chapel to Lincolnshire men. As the buildings share many details, the distinction is perhaps too rigid. It arises in some instances from concentration on either the architecture or the sculpture, but even Prior, who considered both and detected three groups of masons, apparently did not see that they helped or copied one another. Joan Evans also considered both architecture and sculpture, but drew no conclusions,[20] and it is perhaps significant that Webb, the other authority who reached no conclusion, was the only one to comment on the great similarities of detail in the buildings, writing: 'Either one school of masons imitated the other or a single controlling designer dictated to both'.[21] The views expressed by these scholars presuppose that a group of masons may be detected by the individuality of its style, and two scholars, who presumably subscribe to this proposition, add to the complications: Pevsner and Stone suggest that the Lady chapel was abandoned at the fall of the tower and that all hands were put to work on the main building, not returning to the Lady chapel until work on the choir was finished, that is *c*.1336.[22] As this has serious implications for the date of the Lady chapel sculptures, it is of some importance. Although they do not argue their case, we must assume that Pevsner and Stone detected the work of Lady chapel masons throughout the octagon and choir, including the vaulting, and that they saw a consistent style throughout the 14th-century work.

In the following discussion, which has many strands, I shall try to show that the Lady chapel masons were a separate group, whose work is so distinctive that its appearance in the choir can be used to suggest a more exact timetable of work in the Lady chapel, with all that that implies for the date of the sculptures. In order to do this it is necessary to discuss the differences and similarities between the 14th-century buildings and the sources of their styles. The problems posed by the confusion and changes in the choir bays are so crucial that they will be considered in some detail.

The differences between the four main buildings may be explained partly by their different functions. The decoration appropriate to a chapel would be unsuitable on a crossing tower: thus the octagon is relatively plain, while the two chapels have richly moulded interior surfaces. The choir bays have a purely structural purpose in linking the octagon with Northwold's work; they have no specific liturgical function, as the ritual choir ran across the octagon into the choir bays, and neither the octagon nor the bays to its east completely reflected or enclosed the ritual choir. The interior disposition of the choir bays was eventually made to resemble the elevation of Northwold's bays, and while the octagon and the two chapels can each be seen as realised without major breaks, the choir bays contain clear evidence of indecision and changes of design.

Yet, despite the diversity of use, plan and elevation, the buildings have much in common. Webb's idea of a single designer or masonic imitation was based on a feature he found in both chapels and the octagon, 'a three-sided bowed feature, the ogee arches of which suggest the outlines of niches. These are, as it were, drawn over and across the main vaulting shafts which appear rising through and behind them. The same motif appears between the windows of the Lady chapel'.[23] Webb seems to have confused two motifs. The Lady chapel motif is a nodding ogee (Pl. XIIB), bending forward in front of the vaulting shafts, but not designed to conceal them, with wall arches behind it. This motif is not found in the octagon, but Prior Crauden's chapel (Pl. XIIA) has niches with nodding ogees, and an oratory on each side wall, the lower storey of which has a nodding ogee in front of wall arches. These are unrelated to vaulting shafts. The octagon (Pl. XIIIA) has two decorative motifs, both found in the prior's chapel and not connected with the Lady chapel decoration. The feature concealing the vaulting shafts of the octagon is an open triptych, identical to those on the upper storeys of the Crauden oratories. It is intended to hide the change in the number of vaulting shafts from five to three. Under the octagon windows are niches for statues in the form of ogival trefoil shapes, exactly reflecting the motif used for the tracery of the end windows of Prior Crauden's chapel: in the east window it makes a frame round the centrepiece, and in the west window three of them interlock to form the centrepiece. Webb seems to have treated these distinct motifs as one, relating the Lady chapel to the octagon in an untenable way. The two buildings have little in common.

Nevertheless similarities abound in the 14th-century work. The niches with nodding ogees across the corners of the prior's chapel reappear in the Lady chapel to deny the corners in the same way. The eastern bays of the new choir aisles are canted inwards suggesting an attempt to soften the angles. The nodding ogees in Crauden's chapel have a characteristic moulding with an outer cusped layer concealing an inner plain one. This is also used on Hotham's tomb, and seems to be peculiar to Ely. The squared quadrilobe decoration on the oratories reappears as an openwork parapet in the Lady chapel, and the use of overlapping, double mouldings in the bigger chapel was perhaps adumbrated in the smaller. The casement moulding noted by Harvey[24] was used again in the octagon and choir.

The arcades of choir and octagon are very similar (Pl. XIIIA). The arches have two outer orders with seaweed capitals, and an inner order of continuous moulding separated on both sides by a casement moulding. In the octagon this is very narrow, but in the choir it is wider and more emphatic (Pl. XI). These arch mouldings are used in the aisle windows, and the arcade and gallery of the choir, with variations in the capitals which will be discussed later. The choir arches, except in the south aisle, have flower studs on the outer mouldings. In both octagon and choir the continuous mouldings descend to an octagonal base joined to the round bases of the outer mouldings. The round bases have an octagonal band, which is fluted in the south choir aisle. The choir piers and much of the gallery detail are marble, matching the 13th-century building. This is reflected in the use of marble shafts on the octagon windows and the wall-niches of the Lady chapel. The flower-studded mouldings also appear in the Lady chapel, together with fluted shafts and concave-moulded octagonal statue bases. The window tracery, mostly based on a Y-division, with fat, aimless soufflets, is of the same type in the octagon, choir aisles and Lady chapel. The same figure style appears on the sculptures of Hotham's tomb and the Lady chapel, and perhaps on the Etheldreda capitals of the octagon. The lierne vaults of the choir and Lady chapel are clearly related (Fig. 1).

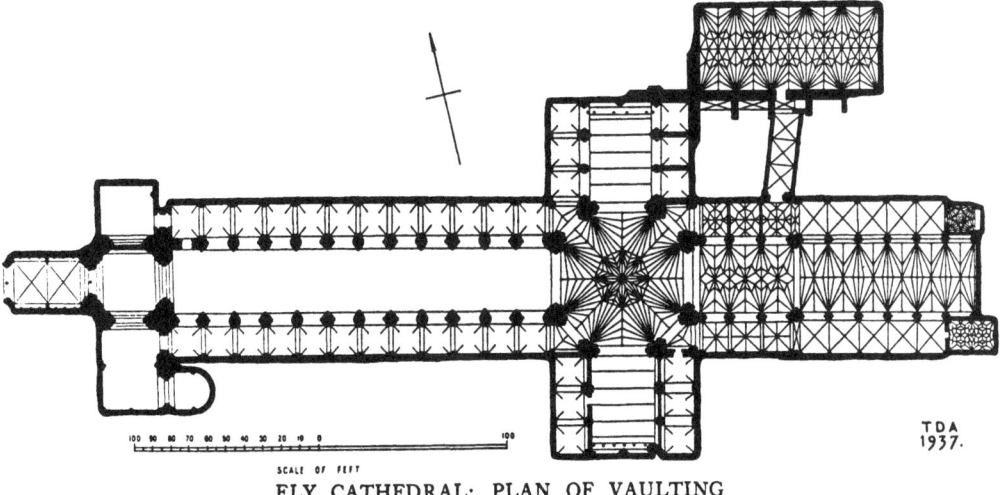

FIG. 1. Diagram of vault patterns *from* VCH, *Cambridge and the Isle of Ely*, IV (1953)

This accumulation of details in common seems to offer overwhelming evidence of one workshop and one designer; but it should be noted that all the details listed above can be copied very easily. Some of the differences in the buildings cannot be explained by their different functions. The tracery and figure sculpture of the octagon may be related to that of the Lady chapel, but they would have been carved *ex situ*. The structure of Prior Crauden's chapel (Pl. XIIA) is essentially different from that of the Lady chapel (Pl. XIIB), with bundles of shafts standing forward from the wall to support the vault, said by Bock to reflect French influence,[25] but possibly related to a similar design in the galilee. The mouldings of Prior Crauden's chapel are heavier and rounder than those of the Lady chapel: there are no concave or octagonal forms, and the arches are unlike those of the octagon or choir.

The choir bays have more than one design, the earliest of which can be seen in the south-west bay of the main elevation (Pl. VIII). All the choir bays have three storeys in proportions matching the 13th-century bays. There is a clerestory passage and a deep, high gallery, both legacies from the Anglo-Norman building. The south-west bay has the same arcade mouldings as the rest, but the spandrels of both arcade and gallery are decorated with shields of arms against a foliate ground. Between this bay and the next is a foliate statue base, built in at gallery level, with a crownlike canopy above at the springing of the vault. It seems to have been planned from the beginning, and while they may have wanted a single statue, it is more likely that the original plan was for a statue under a canopy between every bay. The south-west bay is slightly narrower than the others, so the tracery pattern of the gallery has been modified, but it is fundamentally the same as the rest of the gallery. The gallery capitals are round moulded as in Prior Crauden's chapel, another sign of early work.

The rest of the choir abandoned the shields of arms in favour of a design closer to that of Northwold's work, with long, foliate corbels for the vaulting shafts, and spandrels pierced with cusped, elongated trilobes, a 14th-century version of the 13th-century design. The double shafting of Northwold's clerestory is represented in later bays by a frill of cusping on the inner arch. Capitals and bases are octagonal in the north gallery, mixed, with some fluted, in the south gallery. The tracery is a much-cusped version of the four-petal-flower. The clerestory windows have either convergent or divergent mouchettes. The high vault fits the south-west bay as neatly as the others, and a lierne vault was possibly planned from the beginning. The foreordained height of the choir vault was not taken into account by the designer of the octagon; it is several feet lower than the arch to the octagon, a gap made up with blind tracery on the octagon side.

While the main elevation was built from west to east and from south to north, there are signs in the aisles of a more complicated order of working. The westernmost imposts of the aisle arches are built into the backs of the octagon piers, with marble capitals in a stone pier. The capitals are round moulded, and these piers, both north and south, have a keeled central shaft. The second and third freestanding piers of the south aisle are also keeled, but the north aisle has no other examples. The north-west and south-east bases in the north aisle have fluted bands, as do all the south aisle bases (Pl. X) and some of those in the south gallery; the other north aisle bases are like those of the octagon. The choir bays are separated from the retrochoir by heavy Norman piers surmounted by a 13th-century arch so deep that extra small bays were put into the aisles to bridge the gap there (Pl. X). These bays contain a mixture of old and new work. The south arcade capitals are round moulded with added flower studs, except the most easterly in the narrow bay, which has a unique sixteen-sided abacus. The narrow bay of the north aisle has one stiff-leaf capital on a 13th-century shaft, one capital with a flower-stud moulding and two round moulded capitals like those of the western imposts. One of these is attached to a shaft which supports nothing and seems to be the victim of a change of plan. The other arcade capitals of the north side are moulded with octagonal abaci (Pl. XI), a motif absent from the south arcade.

The narrow bays contain pedestals for statues, bonded in from the base (Pl. X). They have fluted bases, fluted shafts supporting a seaweed corbel with a concave moulded octagonal statue base on it. This piece of marble continues as the adjacent shaft ring. The delicacy of these pedestals can be compared with the sixteen-sided abacus, which is near the one on the south aisle. The pedestals are placed on the piece of wall which is canted inwards at the end of the 14th-century part of the aisle.

While the vault of the north aisle goes with the high vault, and descends to its imposts in the conventional way (Pl. XI), the south aisle vault is a simpler quadripartite rib pattern, with ridge ribs on both axes. As the vault mouldings descend to the imposts they interpenetrate (Pl. X). The ridge ribs of both aisles have flower-studded mouldings.

Some sense can be made of this mixture. The western imposts of both aisles are part of the earliest phase, and the rounded capitals of the south aisle suggest that it is earlier than the north. The narrow bay of the north aisle, with round or flower-studded capitals and a keeled shaft seems to go with the earliest work, and the narrow bays were probably finished in the first phase to smooth off the break at that end. The more elaborate vault of the north aisle is not conclusive evidence of a later date, as the monks may have wanted a more lavish approach to the passage which led from there to the Lady chapel, but the rest of the north aisle has details in common with the second choir elevation. The difference in bases, between fluted and unfluted, remains unexplained, but it is nevertheless possible to suggest a building sequence beginning in the aisles and south-west bay, with the narrow bays, the south aisle perhaps before the north aisle, and the main elevation following.

The stylistic mixture in the choir is as confusing as its relation to other parts of the cathedral. The choir has arch mouldings, some capitals and bases in common with the octagon, but, inevitably, a different vault. The lierne vaults of the choir are similar to that of the Lady chapel, and it is in the Lady chapel that the concave mouldings and thin, delicately fluted supports are also found. Fluted mouldings are used abundantly on the wall shafts at the backs of the stalls (Pl. XVIB). The supports for statues are octagonal, with concave mouldings in the higher niches. Most of the foliage is seaweed.

Two sculptured pieces in the choir are also related to the Lady chapel: the tomb of Bishop Hotham and the north door. Hotham's tomb has panels of blind flowing tracery, convergent mouchettes like the choir clerestory, and the double moulding already noted in Prior Crauden's chapel, but here handled with greater delicacy The only surviving figure of a weeper is by one of the Lady chapel sculptors.[26]

The door leading from the north aisle to the demolished passage to the Lady chapel (Pl. XIIIB) has ogee arches in front of diapered gables; identical statue bases to those of the Lady chapel; and in the moulding of the door jamb, canopied settings for statues, the lowest of which is supported on a thin, fluted colonette, identical to those in the Lady chapel stalls. The censing angels in the diapered spandrels and the mutilated figure seated above the door were by a Lady chapel sculptor. Much of the ornament is on the three-tiered hexagonal niches either side of the door. Open-sided, divided by slender uprights recalling the Hardingstone Cross, they jut forward into the aisle like the nodding ogees of the two chapels.

The tomb, the door and the pedestals in the narrow bays are all by men who worked in the Lady chapel, and their delicate, alien style can also be seen in the fluted bases of the choir and other details of the aisles. The main arcade is not by this group. The tracery is an interesting problem: convergent mouchettes appear in the choir clerestory and Hotham tomb, but not in the Lady chapel, whose tracery is nearer to that of the octagon. The vault patterns, on the other hand, are shared by the choir and Lady chapel to the exclusion of the octagon. These difficulties can eventually be resolved, but they do exemplify one of the greatest problems in studying the decoration of this period, the question of how far any one design was peculiar to one group of masons, or even to one designer, and how far motifs of all kinds were exchanged and copied.

Before deciding who was responsible for what, sources and chronology must be established as far as possible. Spectacular though the octagon and Lady chapel are, they are both part of local tradition, and the presence of someone from London to set out the octagon should not obscure this.[27] This individual is the art historical counterpart of Coleridge's 'man from Porlock', who had a similar decisive effect on the creation of a work of art, but where the man from Porlock halted the composition for ever, the person from London helped it into being. There is little reason to suppose that he was William Hurley. As Pevsner pointed out,[28] the 3*s*. 4*d*. paid to him was not a large sum, and the sacrist was unable to remember his name, hardly a fate to overtake Hurley, who was already a master carpenter by 1323.[29] There is no evidence that Hurley was at Ely before 1325 when the octagon was well launched, and the plan of the building, that of a large chapter house, would not have needed a carpenter's advice. Once set out, the stonework was built within five years, and can have presented few problems. Hurley's role surely began in 1328, when the lantern was begun, supported on a wooden vault ten feet greater in span than the wooden vault of York chapter house; the final *ensemble* somewhat resembled the roof of a kitchen.[30] The huge sum of £8 that Hurley was paid in 1334–35 can only be associated with the lantern, which, according to

Chapman's calculations, was well in hand in that year. The record of payments to Hurley bears this out: his last recorded fee of £8 was paid in 1336–37; in 1339–40 he was paid 6s. 8d., and after that £1 per year until his death, with extra expenses in 1341–42 when he and his assistants were fitting the ritual choir, which he had probably designed and made. The latter payments may be associated with the ritual choir, and probably with a consultant's role in supervising the settlement of the lantern, which caused alarm for the first few years.[31]

The person from London remains unidentified, and as the octagon betrays no knowledge of London work as we know it, the fact that he came from London is probably no more significant than the fact that Thomas Carpenter came from Newport.[32] The Londoner seems to have set out the octagon, and left Ely never to return. The octagonal shape may or may not have been his idea, but it is surely not necessary to adduce the polygonal crossings of Florence and Siena cathedrals as sources of the crossing of Ely; it is very much a building of its time and country.[33] Polygons, both regular and irregular, were being fully exploited in early 14th-century England, following a long tradition in chapter houses, where at least one, Lichfield, is an irregular polygon. We find the same interests explored in castle towers, the Eleanor Crosses and in parts of churches. Although Pevsner believed that the octagonal Norman towers could not have inspired the designer of the octagon,[34] it is quite possible that the Norman crossing had an octagonal lantern over a square crossing, echoed by the sixteen-sided towers on the western transept. The original crossing piers may have been so weakened by the fall of the tower that they had to be completely cleared, and when the time came to rebuild, the octagonal design may have been extended downwards. If it were an idea conceived in Ely itself, the possibility that the sacrist thought of it becomes the greater.[35]

The Lady chapel is in some ways strongly East Anglian. Its position on the corner of the north transept probably owes more to Benedictine practice than East Anglian tradition, but among the comparatively few churches known to have had separate Lady chapels sited to the north or south of the main building, Peterborough and Bury St Edmunds are prominent. Both chapels are destroyed but we know that the Bury chapel was the same width as Ely and some twenty feet shorter.[36] It was decorated with wall and panel paintings of the life and miracles of the Virgin, all of which were used in the larger collection at Ely. They are among very few known examples of Lady chapels thus appropriately adorned, and we may take for granted the model of Bury in the planning of Ely. The cult of the Virgin was flourishing throughout East Anglia at this time: the Bauchun chapel and its northern counterpart were added to the presbytery of Norwich cathedral in the late 1320s, and Miss Dodwell is satisfied that the north chapel was dedicated to St Anne, while the Bauchun chapel carried a dedication to the Virgin.[37]

A group of masons, or a set of designs, can be traced through East Anglia in these years, appearing first at Norwich, then at Ely, Butley and Bury. At Norwich the style appears in the porch of Bishop Salmon's hall and the Bauchun chapel. The styles of Norwich have yet to be properly elucidated; the work in the cloister seems to be by a different group. One may say fairly certainly that the vast programme of rebuilding in the time of Bishop Salmon inspired the work at Ely in the 1320s. In the east porch of Bishop Salmon's hall, c.1319 onwards,[38] they used ogee-headed niches with continuous mouldings, nodding ogees over niches diagonally set, and ogival mouldings as outer rims of main arches. This last feature also appeared in the Bauchun chapel in the late 1320s,[39] where a form of continuous moulding with deep grooves like the octagon and choir arcades of Ely appears on the main arch. The same designs were employed in the later 1320s on the gatehouses of Butley and Bury,[40] and at Butley Caroë noted domical vaulting similar to that of bishop Salmon's porch. The north doors of Butley have continuous mouldings recalling the pattern of Ely and Norwich.[41]

These motifs appear scattered about at Ely. The ogival outer arch moulding is used on the windows and door of the north choir aisle, and the diagonal niches in prior Crauden's chapel. A corner niche on bishop Salmon's porch (Pl. XVIc) has the motif of a nodding ogee with a bar across the top, breaking into the trilobe above. This very curious conceit has an almost identical counterpart in the eastern niche of Prior Crauden's chapel (Pl. XIIA), and its idiosyncrasy suggests the hand of a particular mason. The tracery of the east window of Crauden's chapel recalls, as Pevsner pointed out, the east window of Mildenhall.[42] Harvey's attribution of the prior's chapel and the choir to John Ramsey is founded on the use of casement mouldings in the chapel and the four-petal-flower design of the tracery of the choir gallery and Queen's Hall;[43] both of these motifs are found in the south walk of the Norwich cloister (Pl. XVIA).[44] The Norwich tracery is less elaborate and it preceded Ely, being built 1322–26.[45] The gallery design at Ely is the only tracery which does not have split or double cusping, which Norwich also lacks. The Ethelbert Gate at Norwich, c.1317,[46] has flower-studded arch mouldings, as in the choir and Lady chapel at Ely, a motif still in use at Norwich c.1330 on the Prior's door.[47] The capitals and bases of the Ethelbert Gate are unmatched at Ely, but the vault is an almost identical star pattern to that of the Ely north choir aisle. The vault is generally dated c.1330 by comparison with the undated vault at Ely, but there is no reason why it should not be earlier.[48]

Bishop Salmon built the Carnary as well as the hall, and the interior mouldings of the east window of the Carnary chapel, built by 1316,[49] provide the most likely precedent for the interweaving mouldings of the south choir aisle at Ely. This type of moulding, more popular in the later 14th century, is found in two 13th-century buildings, the cathedrals of Salisbury and Durham. In the latter they are structurally necessary, but at Thornton abbey c.1308,[50] the Carnary chapel and Ely they interweave for decorative effect.

Norwich was not the only source of the styles of Ely, which shares ideas with places much farther afield. Bishop Hotham was a member of an important Yorkshire family which held lands in the district near Selby and Howden, and he was a prebend of York before his elevation to Ely.[51] The shields of arms in the south-west bay of Ely choir have parallels in the nave of York Minster[52] and related buildings before 1315, and the choir of Selby has settings for statues in the spandrels of its arcade.[53] It may be that Selby is just too late to act as a model for Ely, just as the double tracery on the west façade of York Minster and the east façade of Howden may also be later than the double tracery of the octagon windows;[54] but keeled shafts were commonly used in 14th-century Yorkshire, and models for the arcade capitals can also be found there: the round moulded type with flower studs is close to some at Beverley Minster and Patrington, dated before 1320, while the octagonal abaci are used in the nave of York Minster before 1310[55] and in the cloister of Lincoln a little earlier. The settings for statues in the jamb of the north door at Ely are very similar to those in the axial windows of several earlier and contemporary buildings in Yorkshire, for example York Minster, St Mary's abbey, Guisborough and Howden.

Dr R. K. Morris has suggested that the four-petal-flower motif at Bristol may be derived from Norwich or Ely,[56] and ideas seem also to have travelled in the opposite direction. Continuous mouldings are a traditional part of west country architecture, and may be the source of the East Anglian ones, which were used first at Ely.[57] The east wall of the Bristol Lady chapel has a cornice with alternating heads and fleurons remarkably similar to the east wall of the Ely Lady chapel,[58] with, in the tracery above, the square quadrilobe design found at both Norwich and Ely. This wall can be dated before 1322.[59] By the same date the choir of Exeter was exploring themes which recur at Ely:[60] the spandrels of the choir arcade at Ely recall those of the west face of the Exeter pulpitum,[61] the windows at Exeter use a continuous moulding exactly as in the Ely choir and octagon, nodding ogees and jutting three-dimensional designs were present on the bishop's throne and sedilia, and the ogee trilobe shape used in the tracery of Crauden's chapel and in the octagon is hinted at where ogee lancets are combined with trilobes in the window tracery of Exeter choir.[62] Wells and Exeter both use marble for shafting. The lierne vaults of Norwich and Ely may well have come direct from the west country rather than, as Bock suggested,[63] through St Stephen's, Westminster, but it is not easy to say whether a west country mason was prominent in the Ely workforce, or whether Ely masons knew the west country.

The notion that Ely Lady chapel is a version of St Stephen's is attractive. They had in common a rectangular plan, large areas of stained glass and rich coverage of carved and painted decoration. St Stephen's upper chapel dado was well in hand by 1325, and although work was soon interrupted the designs were known.[64] St Stephen's, like Ely, had nodding ogees, illusionistic treatment of the wall shafts and concave moulded statue bases,[65] and Ely has a wave moulding associated by Dr R. K. Morris with the Court masons. Bishop Hotham and Prior Crauden were on friendly terms with members of the Court.[66]

There are objections: St Stephen's was a two-storey *sainte-chapelle* in the tradition of private chapels, while Ely is a single-storey Lady chapel with rectangular precedents other than Westminster. Although Ely workers are recorded at St Stephen's,[67] there is no record of any London mason at Ely apart from the visitor of 1323. Hurley's choir stalls of 'advanced London style'[68] are sufficiently unlike anything else at Ely to call into question Ely's real interest in London styles. As Hurley worked at St Stephen's, we must assume that the royal chapel was in such an advanced style. The Ely Lady chapel is not like the choir stalls. It may therefore have interpreted a London idea, but the masons were not Londoners.

The basis of the decoration in the Lady chapel is the nodding ogee with applied figure sculpture. This may be an exploitation of ideas adumbrated at St Albans, where little figures under nodding ogees appear in the Lady chapel before 1315.[69] A case could be made for the influence of St Albans on Ely: the wooden presbytery vault has the same pattern as the Ely south aisle, with flower studs in the mouldings, and shields of arms at the springing, which could have been translated into the arrangement at Ely. There is a fluted base in the new work of the nave south aisle, c.1324–26, and the shrine of St Alban, 1305–6, has a form of fluted shaft.[70] It is, however, rather half-hearted, and Ely almost certainly drew its ideas from elsewhere.

The only fluted decoration certainly earlier than St Albans and Ely is in St Hugh's choir at Lincoln.[71] Although it is many years earlier, its type of decoration remains the nearest precedent; in the intervening years the decoration of the flat wall surface had prevailed, and Ely was here reviving the habit of decorating the architectural members. Octagonal abaci are also found at Lincoln, and the concave-moulded octagons of Ely may also be drawn from there. Scholars are agreed that Lincolnshire supplied the figure style at Ely.

The Lady chapel masons may have carved the capitals, head-stops and high boss of the octagon, but the corbels in the two monastic halls were possibly by a different group.[72] The surviving figure sculpture of the Lady chapel is on the stalls, and it resembles a tapestry or manuscript, with coloured figures against a gilt diaper background, and priestly witnesses in the stalls and on finials, similar to those in niches in, for example, Queen Mary's Psalter.[73] The iconography cannot be discussed here, but the narrative cycle itself needs comment.[74] Sculptured cycles, whether or not in spandrels, are hard to find at this date, although painted sequences are common. The chapter house of Salisbury is the nearest surviving precedent for narrative sculpture in spandrels. Isolated scenes occur on, for example, the shrine of St Alban and the stone Easter sepulchres of the Lincolnshire group; but these, considerations of date apart, are not narrative cycles. The shrine of St Alban has scenes on the end gables, with censing angels or single figures in the spandrels. The bosses in the cloister at Norwich and the capitals in the octagon at Ely are nearer both in time and space than Salisbury, and are genuine narrative sequences. The Passion series in the east walk at Norwich were probably made c.1316–30[75] and the Etheldreda capitals c.1325.

Norwich was not, however, the source of the figure style. The carvers of the east cloister walk and Prior's door made admirable foliage and told their stories with economy and vigour. Their figure style, with large heads, hands and feet, awkward gestures and coarse, weightless draperies, is very poor.[76] The Etheldreda capitals at Ely slightly reflect the Norwich attributes, telling their story with equal vigour and producing quite well-executed foliage in the scene where the saint's staff takes root and blossoms (Pl. XIVc). The figures are more tranquil than those of Norwich and have more natural proportions. The draperies loop in heavy curves.

The master sculptor of the Lady chapel, and even his assistants, carved figures of a litheness and grace not matched in the octagon and beyond the powers of the Norwich cloister sculptors. The Ely workshop enjoyed the bulk and texture of drapery for their own sake. The master's hand may be seen in The Presentation of the Virgin (Pl. XIVA): both the long curve of the figures and the perspective handling of the flight of steps are inconceivable at Norwich.

The heavy, graceful style of Ely, with overlapping pleats and long, weighty curves, is, as Prior and Gardner pointed out many years ago,[77] the style of the Lincolnshire masons. It is first apparent on the Lincoln Easter sepulchre, a work normally dated to the 1290s.[78] Pevsner compares the sepulchre to the cloister, both having the sophisticated mouldings and tracery characteristic of London work in the late 13th century. A date about ten years later is quite possible. The figure style is not typical of London styles as we know them. Richard of Stow, employed by the King to make the Lincoln Eleanor Cross,[79] may have introduced the style to Lincoln, but this we shall never know. In any case it was, and remained, provincial. London draperies, from the Crouchback tomb onwards, skim smoothly over the surface of the body and fall in straight, shallow folds.

Stone believed diaper to be characteristic of London rather than Lincoln, but that only Lincolnshire masons were sufficiently experienced in carved screen work to have produced the Ely Lady chapel.[80] By this date diaper was well dispersed in the provinces, on the Crosses at Waltham and Geddington, at Beverley and Howden, and was also used on the pulpita of Lincoln and Southwell and the Hawton Easter sepulchre, although these are not of certain date.

The objects closest in style to Ely are the Easter sepulchres at Navenby[81] and Hawton.[82] The Navenby figures have the same lavish drapery and curved pose, and the soldiers wear the same belted tunic as many of the Ely figures. In addition, the east window of the church has an elaborate version of the ogival trilobes of Prior Crauden's chapel, with a series of divergent mouchettes and split cusps, assembled in a pattern which looks more developed than Ely. To date tracery on visual evidence alone is notoriously unreliable, but if the two are connected, Ely is probably earlier. Hawton makes full use of the decorative repertory at Ely: nodding ogees, bead-and-reel ornament and diaper work including naturalistic roses. The double ogee arches of the piscina enter the moulding of the containing arch in exactly the same way as at Ely. Several hands worked at Hawton: the pelican on the sedilia is not by an Ely sculptor, and the faces of the sleeping soldiers are closer to caricature.[83] However, the surviving figure of a saint in priest's clothes on the sedilia may be by the same hand as the surviving finial priest at Ely; the left-hand apostle in the Hawton Ascension is identical in pose, with body tilted forward and foot flat on the ground, to some of the apostles in procession at Ely (Pl. XIVB). The larger figures have draperies of squarer cut and harder edge than Ely, but their greater size may explain the difference. The workforce at Hawton surely included some who worked at Ely.[84]

None of the Lincolnshire monuments is securely dated. The Lincoln sepulchre is much earlier than Ely, but the relative dating of Ely on the one hand, and Heckington, Hawton, Navenby and the screen of Lincoln and Southwell on the other, is uncertain. Navenby and the two screens have no date. Heckington chancel was fitted out by the priest Richard of Potesgrave, 1307–36; these dates encompass Ely.[85] Nor is the date of Hawton entirely certain. The tomb in the chancel is said to be that of Sir Robert de Compton, *d*.1330, but it is not clear whether he fitted out the chancel before he died, or whether his heirs made it a memorial chapel to him.[86] At this stage, given the chronological difficulties in Ely itself, a sequence of work in the two areas could only be postulated.

At Ely, the Norwich group were largely responsible for the octagon, the choir bays and Prior Crauden's chapel, while the men of the north-east concentrated on the Lady chapel. In view of the shared links of both figure-sculpture and decorative mouldings with the north-east we can assume that the same group was responsible for both, and that Lincolnshire men were not confined to the figure sculpture while Londoners did the rest. Both groups of masons used some motifs of the other, and each had a hand in the buildings of the other.

We know that the Lady chapel masons provided some of the decorative work in the choir, and they may have designed the oratories and triptych designs for the octagon and Crauden's chapel. These pieces are more at home in the Lincolnshire repertoire. Conversely the Norwich masons may have vaulted the Lady chapel and put the windows in. Neither the vault nor the tracery of the Lady chapel is a Lincolnshire type.

The chronology of the choir and Lady chapel, and Ely's relationship to the north-east give some support to this view. The Lady chapel style can be traced in the following works in the choir: the pedestals in the narrow bays, the fluted bases, the Hotham tomb and the north door. The masons may also have been responsible for the early phase of work in the south-east bay, the south aisle and the octagonal capitals in the north aisle. It is reasonable to suppose that northerly masons could have brought Yorkshire ideas, perhaps at the instigation of Hotham. It is less reasonable to suppose that a group of Yorkshire masons appeared briefly and went away again, although given the evident lack of direction in the choir, such a solution is not wholly impossible. The pedestals in the narrow bays are bonded in and must date from the earliest phase. The other architectural pieces could have been left ready for use, and the tomb and door made at any time within the building period of the choir. The longest job would have been the building of the south-east bay, but there is no doubt that it went up first.

Work was in progress in the Lady chapel in 1323. The relief sculptures are in the lower wall, physically part of it, being put in as the wall rose. The number of incompetent joins shows that the carving was done *ex situ*. Above the level of the stalls is the entire superstructure of the Lady chapel, including a vault forty feet wide, which cannot have been easy to put up. Yet the roof must have been on and at least some of the scaffolding down by 1345 when Bishop Montacute was buried in the chapel. Pevsner sees a break in the building above the zone of the marble (the sculptures come above the break),[87] but the change from marble surely reflects current taste: the tomb of Edward II, the shrine of St Alban, the Wells Lady chapel, the Exeter pulpitum, the Beverley reredos and the choir of Ely itself all combine stone with greater or smaller amounts of marble, used mostly for shaft work as in the Lady chapel. Its absence higher in the Lady chapel need not denote a change of plan, or break. We know that the Lady chapel masons worked in the choir at the beginning and at some unspecified time. We also know that there was a workforce at Ely large enough for the sacrist constantly to build offices and workshops all over the precinct while the *novum opus* was in progress.[88] Logic suggests that the lower wall of the Lady chapel was ready in reasonable time. It seems likely that the relatively small amount of Lady chapel work in the choir did not seriously disrupt progress on the Lady chapel; all the sculptures were probably made in the mid-1320s, and the choir door and tomb followed soon after.[89] The Lincolnshire masons could have been moving homewards by the early 1330s, leaving the vault and windows to be made by the Norwich men. The sculpture style of the Lady chapel vault bosses is closer in quality to the Norwich cloister than to the spandrel figures below.

The reason for the foregoing discussion is that the Sacrist Rolls do not exist for the crucial decade of 1325–34, and even where they do exist they record only the purchase of materials and the problems of everyday administration. They enabled Chapman to work out a convincing chronology for the new work, but they rarely say where a mason came from, and even more rarely do they give his full name. Rolls exist for the years between 1322 and 1358, but serious building work stopped in 1345–46, and for the quarter of a century after 1322 there survive eight annual rolls, for the years 1322–25 inclusive, 1334–35, 1336–37, 1339–40, 1341–42, 1345–46. All information about the masons comes from the Rolls, and with no information between 1325 and 1334 we are in difficulties. We know nothing of the masons of the two chapels, as they were not the sacrist's responsibility.

We cannot check the most problematical part of the building against the documents. The early design of the choir demonstrates the difficulties. The arcade and exterior wall are both Norwich designs. Into this was inserted one bay of the elevation and some capitals resembling work in Yorkshire. These were then abandoned in favour of the Norwich style, with little touches from the Lincolnshire masons. Who made these changes of plan? One answer would be, the bishop; but, although we know that 'the bishop's men' existed, we find them mentioned in 1323–24,[90] at a time when the Norwich men are more likely to have been in charge. They may have been so designated because the bishop was paying them, and not because they were a separate group. They are not mentioned the next year, and after that comes the break in the records. All we know is that the choir was subject to successive changes of design, but we do not know if there were successive changes of architect in the early days. Nor do we know the identity of the architect, if such he can be called.

Several masons were named in the first three years: John the Mason, Peter Quadratarius and 'cuidam de Londonia'. Thomas Carpenter was putting up scaffolding.[91] After the interval of ten years there had been a complete change. No mason was named under the *novum opus*, but the new carpenter, William Hurley, was in receipt of his enormous £8 fee.[92] In 1336–37 the mason in charge of the new work was John Attegrene, who had been at Ely the year before but not employed on the new work. We do not know when he first appeared at Ely, but he travelled between Ely and Norwich.[93] His Norwich commitments suggest that he cannot have given full attention to either place and he seems to have come to the new work too late to have had much effect on the design.

The careers of the other Ely masons are far less certain, and their appearances in the surviving documents are fleet. Peter Quadratarius is not mentioned after 1323 and he may have been an early consultant. The man from London has already been discussed. The fact of his visit calls into question the competence of Master John the Mason. This figure has been identified by Harvey as John Ramsey of Norwich, acting as a consultant architect to Ely, as he was paid a fee as well as wages.[94] This view fits Ramsey's known activities in the cloister of Norwich from 1322–26,[95] and possibly explains why John the Mason was not at Ely in 1324–25 (the break in the records after that date making him disappear from Ely after 1323). It also explains why the choir bays seem to lack the guidance of a strong hand. However, as has been pointed out above, Master John's incompetence or unwillingness to set out the octagon suggests that he was not a master of note. As Harvey has shown, many masons were called John.[96] The groups of masons who built Ely apparently built no monumental architecture apart from Ely, and were apparently unused to building it. The Norwich group built small gatehouses and simple halls; the Lincolnshire group were mason-decorators, who did not tackle vaults, and were certainly not the architects of great churches. Now it is possible that John Ramsey himself was just such a mason-decorator. Ely lacks the unifying vision of the true architect. Of the two buildings with the least applied decoration, one was set out by a visiting master and the other was subject to changes of design throughout its history. Before the fall of the tower, masons who specialised in tombs, Easter sepulchres and other essentially sculptural objects were called in to build the Lady chapel, a simple box with lavish applied decoration. The sculptured enrichment is confidently handled and of high quality, carried out by men who knew what they were doing. The other conventual buildings are of simple design with good sculpture. The master masons do not seem to have produced a coherent architectural idea, but rather a series of beautifully decorated solutions to individual problems. This may be the style of John Ramsey.[97]

Thus, the styles of Ely are mixed, but not inextricably entwined. The East Anglian style predominates in the choir, octagon and prior Crauden's chapel, and the Lincolnshire style predominates in the Lady chapel. Someone knew of recent developments in Yorkshire and the west country. It seems likely that the Norwich masons finished the Lady chapel and the Lincolnshire masons helped in the other parts of the building, but they were hired to build their particular parts, and there were no long breaks while all concentrated on one building. Some of the ideas at Ely are based on earlier work in the church, and the buildings give the impression that the monks thought in local terms. They do not seem to have been interested in using the latest ideas from London or the Court, and they used experts from there only when difficulties arose that the mason-decorators were unable to solve. The monks wanted a lavishly decorated building, and they went to those who could supply it. It would seem reasonable to suppose that the two main styles of Ely represent two groups of masons; but either was presumably able to copy the motifs of the other, and those who wish to identify a design with a particular mason or group, and those who prefer to see ideas spread through notebooks and imitation may use the Decorated work of Ely in their arguments with equal justification.

REFERENCES

SHORTENED TITLES USED

BOCK — H. Bock, *Der Decorated Style* (Heidelberg 1962).
EMA — J. H. Harvey, *English Medieval Architects* (London 1954).
EVANS — J. Evans, *English Art 1307–1461* (Oxford 1949).
FERNIE and WHITTINGHAM — E. C. Fernie and A. B. Whittingham, *The Early Communar... Rolls of Norwich Cathedral Priory ...* (Norfolk Record Society, XLI), 1972.
HARVEY, 'Origins of Perp' — J. H. Harvey, 'The origins of the Perpendicular style', in E. M. Jope, ed., *Studies in Building History* (London 1961), 134–65.
Medieval Architect — J. H. Harvey, *The Medieval Architect* (London 1972).
STONE — L. Stone, *Sculpture in Britain: The Middle Ages*, 2nd ed. (Harmondsworth 1972).
WEBB — G. Webb, *Architecture in Britain: The Middle Ages*, 2nd ed. (Harmondsworth 1965).

1. Bentham; Stewart; Ladds; VCH, *Cambridge and the Isle of Ely*, IV (1953); B/E *Cambridgeshire*, 2nd ed. (1970), all give details of plans and general appearance, and discuss several structural problems which will not be reconsidered here. For alterations in the gallery see P. Draper, 'Bishop Northwold and the Cult of St Etheldreda', above pp. 8–27.
2. F. R. Chapman, *The Sacrist Rolls of Ely*, 2 vols (Cambridge 1907).
3. *Anglia Sacra*, I, 644.
4. Chapman, II, 73, 98.
5. Chapman, II, 109, 122.
6. Chapman, II, 83; *Anglia Sacra*, I, 647.
7. Chapman, II, 114–18.
8. Chapman, II, 47.
9. Chapman, I, 51; II, 83.
10. Chapman, II, 28, 29, 32.
11. VCH, *Cambridge and the Isle of Ely*, IV (1953), 62; Harvey, 'Origins of Perp', 136.
12. Chapman, II, 155.
13. Ladds, 8.
14. Chapman, I, 126; Ladds, 8; Stewart, 244; B/E *Cambridgeshire*, 2nd ed. (1970), 374.
15. Chapman, I, 12; Stewart, 84.
16. Chapman, I, 13.
17. Stewart, 137, quoting *Anglia Sacra*, I, 651.
18. Harvey, 'Origins of Perp'; E. S. Prior and A. Gardner, *An account of Medieval Figure Sculpture in England* (Cambridge 1912), 372; Stone, 169–70; E. S. Prior, *The Cathedral Builders in England* (London 1905), 75.
19. EMA, 142; Chapman, II, 45.
20. Evans, 33–34.
21. Webb, 127.
22. B/E *Cambridgeshire*, 2nd ed. (1970), 359; Stone, 170.
23. Webb, 127.
24. Harvey, 'Origins of Perp', 150.
25. Bock, 114.
26. Bentham, pl. XVIII (Pl. XVIIB). The so-called canopy from Hotham's tomb did not in my opinion originally belong to it. Chapman (I, 98) believed it was the base of St Etheldreda's shrine. Ladds (p. 14) related it to the tomb, but admitted that the tomb was longer than the canopy, that the tomb fitted only if it was built into the wall as shown in Bentham's plate, and

that, had there been an effigy, the canopy would have sat very low over it. Both the canopy and the tomb are designed to stand free, and the tomb must have been built into the wall at a later date. It surely stood clear of the choir screen. The canopy is decorated with sculptures of a coarser and stiffer style than that of the tomb. It is probably a 14th-century replacement of the 13th-century base of the shrine, perhaps put in because the new screen and stalls were taller than the old and obscured the shrine. Many shrine bases were being renewed at this time; see N. Coldstream, 'English Decorated Shrine Bases', *JBAA*, CXXIX, 1976, 15–34.

27. Chapman, II, 45.
28. B/E *Cambridgeshire*, 2nd ed. (1970), 356.
29. EMA, 142.
30. Prior, *Cathedral Builders*, 75.
31. EMA, 142–43; Chapman, II, 73, 84, 98, 119 etc.
32. Chapman, II, 29.
33. B/E *Cambridgeshire*, 2nd ed. (1970), 356; Bock, 115–16.
34. B/E *Cambridgeshire*, 2nd ed. (1970), 355–56.
35. Ibid.; *Medieval Architect*, 82; VCH, *Cambridge and the Isle of Ely*, IV (1953), 62; Chapman, I, 69–70; Bentham, 283, are all attracted by the idea that Alan of Walsingham thought of the octagon, an idea hinted in *Anglia Sacra*. Alan was certainly remembered by the chronicler, but his excellence as a sacrist with the interests of the monastery at heart, well attested in the Sacrist Rolls, would have ensured that.
36. VCH, *Cambridge and the Isle of Ely*, IV, 60; A. B. Whittingham, *Bury St Edmunds Abbey*, HMSO (1971); M. R. James, *On the abbey church of St Edmund at Bury* (Cambridge 1895), 142–43.
37. B. Dodwell, 'William Bauchun and his connection with the cathedral priory at Norwich', *Norfolk Archaeology*, XXXVI (1975), 111–12.
38. J. T. Macnaughton-Jones, 'St Ethelbert's Gate, Norwich', *Norfolk Archaeology*, XXXIV (1966), 77.
39. Fernie and Whittingham, 26.
40. W. D. Caroë, 'Butley Priory, Suffolk', *Archaeol. J.*, XC (1933), 239–40.
41. Ibid., pl. IV.
42. B/E *Suffolk* (1961), pl. 7.
43. Atkinson, pl. XXIII.
44. Harvey, 'Origins of Perp', 150; EMA, 150.
45. Fernie and Whittingham, 34.
46. Ibid., 33; Macnaughton-Jones, op. cit., 74–84, pl. 6.
47. Fernie and Whittingham, 34; Stone, pl. 127.
48. Fernie and Whittingham, 33; Macnaughton-Jones, op. cit., 76. While ideas probably travelled between Norwich and Ely in both directions with such masons as John Attegrene, most of them seem to have come from Norwich. The attribution of the Ethelbert vault to William Ramsey, thus forcing a date of c.1330 (EMA, 215; Macnaughton-Jones, op. cit., 77), ignores the possibility that the chapel he was building at the time could have been either of the two presbytery chapels. Although the vault of the gate seems to be a later addition, it need not be as late as 1330.
49. Fernie and Whittingham, 33.
50. A. W. Clapham and K. Major, 'Thornton', *Archaeol. J.*, CIII (1947), 172–78.
51. *Dictionary of National Biography*, XXVII (London 1891), 407–08.
52. Evans, pl. 21.
53. E. S. Prior, *A History of Gothic Art in England* (London 1900), fig. 282.
54. Evans, pl. 20; Webb, pl. 141b. See N. Coldstream, 'York Minster and the Decorated Style in Yorkshire; architectural reaction to York in the first half of the fourteenth century', *Yorkshire Archaeological Journal*, forthcoming.
55. G. E. Aylmer and R. Cant, ed., *A History of York Minster* (Oxford 1978), 155, pl. 50.
56. R. K. Morris, *Decorated Architecture in Herefordshire*, unpublished doctoral thesis for the University of London (1972), 51.

57. Myres's date of 1311–32 for the Butley Gatehouse seems a little early: *Archaeol. J.*, XC (1933), 186.
58. Bock, pl. 39.
59. N. Pevsner, 'Bristol, Troyes, Gloucester', *Architectural Review*, CXIII (1953), 90.
60. Webb, 137.
61. Harvey, 'Origins of Perp', 150; Bock, pl. 46.
62. J. Britton, *Cathedral Antiquities*, IV (London 1834), Exeter, pl. XII, especially nos. 9 and 11, where the ogees are helped a little.
63. Bock, 54.
64. H. M. Colvin, ed., *History of the King's Works*, I (London 1963), 514–17.
65. Bock, fig. 18.
66. Stewart, 83, 84.
67. W. Stevenson, *Supplement and Notes to Bentham's Ely* (Norwich 1817), 64.
68. EMA, 143.
69. VCH, *Hertfordshire*, II (1908), 490.
70. EMA, 307; VCH, *Hertfordshire*, II (1908), 486.
71. Prior, *History of Gothic Art*, figs 75, 121; F. Bond, *Gothic Architecture in England* (London 1905), 249. Thornton has a fluted base of c.1325, and Chepstow castle some fluted consoles of uncertain 14th-century date.
72. Atkinson, pl. XXII. They are far closer to models from life, which would not in itself argue a different hand, but a head in Bishop Salmon's porch closely resembles them, and as the Norwich group seems to have worked on the conventual buildings at Ely, they may have made the corbels for the halls.
73. G. F. Warner, ed., *Queen Mary's Psalter* (London 1912), pl. 147 et pass.
74. For the iconography see M. R. James, *The Sculptures in the Lady Chapel at Ely* (London 1895).
75. Fernie and Whittingham, 33.
76. Illustrated in G. Thurlow, *Norwich Cathedral* (Norwich 1972), 72.
77. Prior and Gardner, *Medieval Figure Sculpture*, 372; Stone, 169–70. I use the term 'Lincolnshire' to include works by the same people in Nottinghamshire.
78. B/E *Lincolnshire* (1964), 114; Stone, 168.
79. Colvin, *King's Works*, I, 483.
80. Stone, 169–70.
81. Prior and Gardner, *Medieval Figure Sculpture*, 368.
82. Stone, pl. 125.
83. Stone, 169, pl. 128.
84. I have benefited from discussion of the Lincolnshire sculptures with Miss Veronica Sekules, but the opinions here expressed are my own.
85. C. A. Norris, 'Heckington Church', *JBAA*, New series, XXVII (1921), 81.
86. F. H. Burnside, 'Hawton Church and Newark Museum', *Transactions of the Thoroton Society*, XXIX (1925), 182–88, favours the latter interpretation.
87. B/E *Cambridgeshire* (1970), 359.
88. Chapman, II, passim.
89. This is supported by Harvey's early date for the wall niches of the Lady chapel: Harvey, 'Origins of Perp', 136.
90. Chapman, II, 47.
91. Chapman, I, 21, 22, et pass.; II, 29, 33, 45, etc.; EMA, 142, 150; *Medieval Architect*, 131–32, 178–79.
92. Chapman, II, 73.
93. Chapman, I, 36: II, 68, 84; EMA, 119; Fernie and Whittingham, 37.
94. EMA, 150.
95. Fernie and Whittingham, 34.
96. EMA, Key to Christian Names, 321–22.
97. One Ramsey is mentioned in the Ely records: a William Ramsey, who repaired old windows in 1336–37. He was not concerned in the new work, nor was he named as Master. Harvey gives us

three, or possibly two, Ramseys to choose from (EMA, 215), but the only possible candidate would be William I, who seems not to have had a very successful career. William II is not recorded after 1331, and William III was far too eminent by 1336 to be doing odd repair jobs at Ely. Harvey suggested that William I and William II may have been the same person. William I was Master by 1336, William II by 1326. If it is accepted that the records do not always refer to Masters as such (John Attegrene was not called Master in the Sacrist Roll for 1341–42: the records are not an entirely trustworthy guide to masonic careers), the William at Ely could be William I/II. He may alternatively be a William Ramsey IV, making a lone appearance in the records. It is ironical that the only Ramsey with a documented connection with Ely should appear in so lowly a capacity, and not on the *novum opus*.

The Fourteenth-Century Tile Pavements in Prior Crauden's Chapel and in the South Transept

By LAURENCE KEEN[1]

PRIOR CRAUDEN'S CHAPEL

The tile pavement in Prior Crauden's chapel is not only one of the most celebrated of medieval tile pavements in Britain but is one which received the attention of 18th- and early 19th-century antiquaries at the time when the study of medieval tiles was in its infancy. Richard Gough's account of it was published in 1792,[2] William Fowler published a plan of it in 1801[3] (Pl. XX) and in 1803 W. Wilkins's detailed architectural account of the chapel appeared with a coloured plan of the pavement.[4] Since the publication of these accounts the pavement has been frequently referred to in print, but no detailed description or discussion has yet been attempted.

The pavement covers the whole floor area of the chapel, about 8.50 m east–west, 4.18 m north–south. The sanctuary and the narrow step below it are both at a higher level than the main area of the chapel which occupies an area 6.15 m by 4.18 m. The south-west corner and part of the panel against the north wall have been disturbed by the staircase and fireplace, inserted when the chapel was converted into a dwelling-house.[5] However, the pavement has fortunately suffered little from this secular use.

The decorative effect of the pavement is achieved by the use of tile mosaic, that is, the use of shaped tiles of different colours, combined to produce patterns of varying degrees of complexity.[6] Some of the tiles are decorated with small line-impressed stamps. These two techniques combine to produce a *line-impressed mosaic* pavement. However, not all of the mosaic designs use geometric shapes: several panels incorporate tiles making up naturalistic shapes with *hand-incised* decoration. Hand-incised decoration is also used on square and diamond-shaped tiles with two-colour designs of lions, stags and a bird with spread wings.

The layout of the pavement is complex, as will be seen in Pl. XX. The main area of the pavement is divided into three panels. The north and south panels (0.97 to 0.98 m wide) use the same mosaic design, a small dark coloured roundel with a yellow mosaic five-foil centre, surrounded by a narrow yellow circular tile. This is connected to the next roundel by a small dark coloured circular tile and the spaces between the roundels are filled by dark tiles with four concave sides, a small yellow four-foil tile placed in the centre. The central panel (1.37 to 1.39 m wide) consists of roundels with a small five-foil set into each one, surrounded by narrow circular tiles which intertwine around the connecting small roundels, so forming a single-strand interlace running continuously throughout the panel. The remaining spaces are filled with tiles of eight concave sides set with a large four-foil. The colour arrangement is not so clear in this panel but it seems probable that the interlace motif, and the five and four-foils were yellow and the remaining roundels dark. These three panels are separated by narrow bands 0.27 m wide containing small six-pointed stars. Against both the north and south walls are square and diamond-shaped tiles decorated with birds, stags and lions. The animals are in white slip, appearing yellow under the glaze, and all have hand-incised decoration which provides the details of hips, shoulders etc.

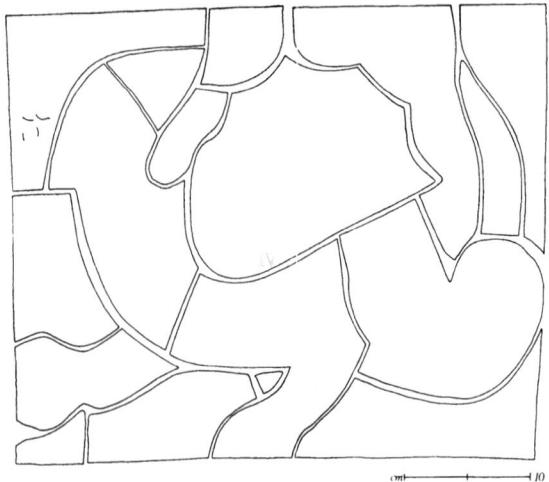

FIG. 1.   Prior Crauden's chapel, small gryphon at W end (4)

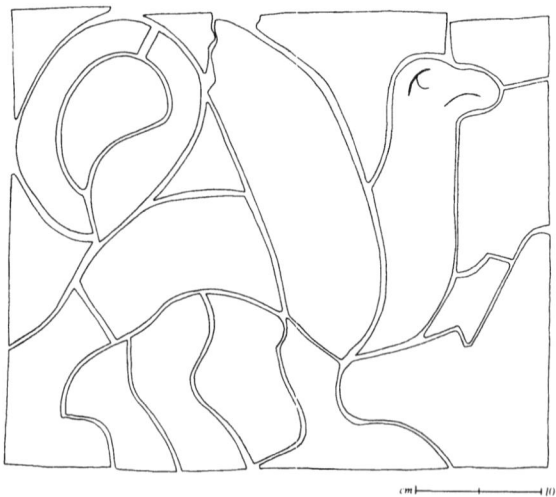

FIG. 2.   Prior Crauden's chapel, small wyvern beneath sanctuary step (3)

Along the west wall and next to the step are two sets of different sized panels. Those along the west wall consist of (from north to south): (1) a large *lion passant guardant*, head to viewer's left; (2) a small *lion passant*, head to left; (3) a small *lion passant*, head to left;[7] (4) a small gryphon facing right (Fig. 1); (5) a small *lion passant*, head to right;[7] (6) a small *lion passant*, head to right. The final panel no longer exists. Beneath the sanctuary step is a similar series. From north to south the panels are: (1) a large *lion passant guardant*, head to right; (2) a large *lion passant*, head to left; (3) a small wyvern (Fig. 2); (4) a large *lion passant*, head to right (Fig. 3); (5) a large *lion passant guardant*, head to left. All these lions are composed of a number of different shaped mosaic elements to produce a striking yellow animal surrounded in its own panel by dark background tiles. It is clear that the mosaic tiles for the lions were made of ordinary red fabric tiles, coated before firing with a layer of white slip to which all the body details, eyes, teeth, tongue, mane, tail etc. were added by hand-incised lines. All the eyes are made from darker clay inlaid into the tile and it should be noted that in a number of cases the mosaic outline of the feet has been reduced in size by scraping away the white slip to form a smaller foot. A coating of lead glaze produced a brilliant yellow after firing. Despite wear, the surviving material demonstrates the extraordinary artistic and technical accomplishment of the tile-makers. An additional fact about the techniques of manufacture becomes apparent if the mosaic elements of what appear to be six different lions are examined in detail. Such an examination shows that only *three* designs are used, each one being reversed to produce a

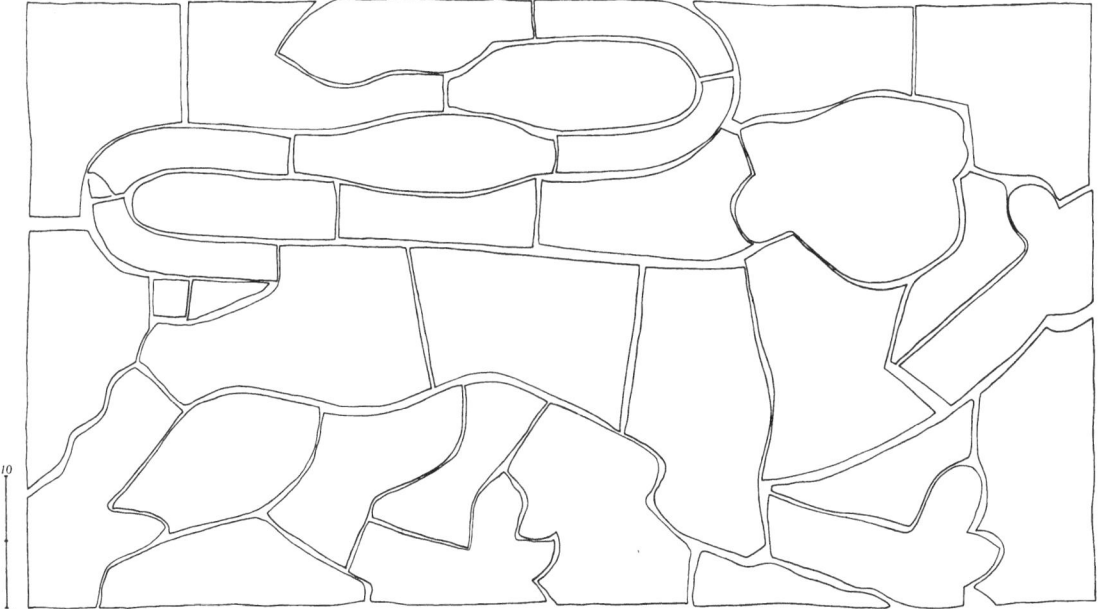

FIG. 3. Prior Crauden's chapel, large *lion passant* beneath sanctuary step (4)

lion facing in the opposite direction. The close correspondence between each mosaic element suggests that templates were used for cutting out each element and that all the templates were reversed to produce lions facing the other way.

A small narrow step decorated with a band of six-pointed stars, divides the main floor of the chapel from the sanctuary. A number of decorative arrangements are found in the sanctuary. It is clear that there must have been a movable altar as the entire sanctuary is paved. In front of the space occupied by the altar is a panel 0.83 m by 1.12 m containing a representation of the temptation of Adam and Eve (Fig. 4). A drawing of this panel was published by Gough in his paper in *Archaeologia* for 1792 and since then the panel has received particular attention. The panel shows Eve on the left-hand side, Adam on the right, with a tree between them. The tree has the serpent twined around it, clusters of fruit on either side and rudimentary foliage. Eve holds fruit in either hand, that in the left hand immediately in front of the serpent's head. The naked figures of Adam and Eve are shown by yellow tiles, and so is the serpent. The tree and its foliage is made of olive green tiles. The panel is made up of a very large number of mosaic elements and it is evident that there was originally much more hand-incised decoration than can be seen now. All three faces have hand-incised detail and Eve's eyes have been made from a dark clay, in the same way as for the lions. Hand-incised detail has also been used to show the individual leaves of the foliage.

On either side of this panel are bands containing a mosaic design of large six-pointed stars arranged around plain hexagons. The space between these bands and the walls is taken up by more lions. On the north, nearest the step, there is a large *lion passant guardant* with head to the right (Fig. 5) and above it, to the east,

FIG. 5. Prior Crauden's chapel, large *lion passant guardant*, sanctuary N side

two smaller lions facing each other (the south one: Fig. 6). On the south, nearest the step, there is a large *lion passant* with head to the left, and above it, to the east, two smaller lions facing each other. All the lions in the sanctuary have the same overall designs as those described above and were clearly made from the same templates: the only variations are found in the hand-incised details. The remaining area of the sanctuary is filled by large six-pointed stars placed around a hexagon and surrounded by narrow tiles with line-impressed decoration, and under the altar a small panel of roundels identical to the two side panels in the main floor.

Date

The Treasurer's accounts for the period Michaelmas 1324 to Michaelmas 1325 record that £138 8s. 5d. was paid *in noua constructione capelle et camere Domini Prioris*.[8] Although the pavement may not have formed part of this work and may have been laid after the chapel was built it seems most likely that a date of 1324–25 is appropriate.

The Pavement and its Setting

A preliminary examination of this pavement brings a number of crucial factors to light. The most important is that the Adam and Eve panel is quite out of place in the overall decorative scheme. Furthermore, it has been observed that in a number of instances the original designs for the three types of lion appear to have been amended by being made somewhat smaller, and, particularly in the sanctuary, the various panels of different designs seem to be far from well laid out and

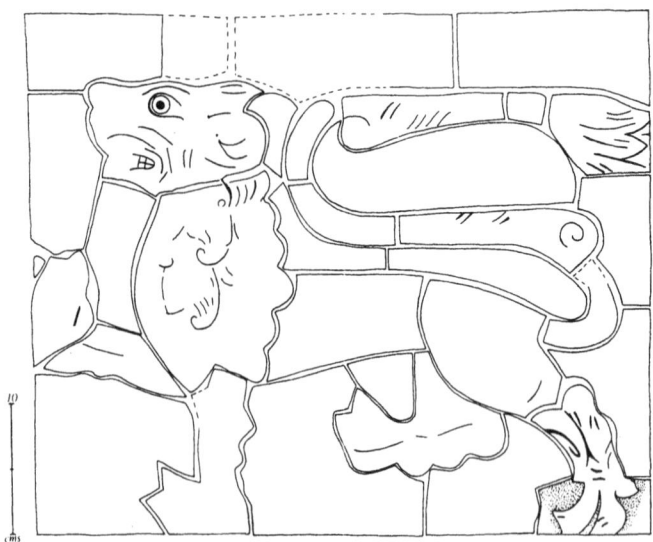

FIG. 6. Prior Crauden's chapel, small *lion passant*, sanctuary N side

organised. These factors lead the writer to suggest that neither the Adam and Eve panels, nor the lions, were intended for this chapel. The pavement may be considered as the 'left-overs' of a much more elaborate pavement. If this hypothesis is accepted the questions of for where, and when was the main pavement designed, must be posed. It has been suggested that in its present arrangement the Adam and Eve panel is out of place. It is out of scale with the rest of the arrangement, not only in size, but in its artistic accomplishment. Furthermore, it is reasonable to suppose that such an elaborate panel formed part, or was intended to form part, of a major iconographical sequence. Eve as a type of the Virgin would not be out of place in a Lady chapel. Furthermore, it is also of interest to note that lions, two on each step of the six steps up to the throne, form part of the representations of the Virgin on the throne of Solomon.[9] The Lady chapel at Ely was started in 1321 when John Crauden was prior, and a central vault boss shows an Adam and Eve scene. It seems most reasonable, therefore, to suggest that a large and elaborate pavement containing a set of panels showing an iconographical scheme related to the Virgin, a series of lions, and panels of intricate mosaic was designed for the Lady chapel. When the central tower fell in 1322, this elaborate and, no doubt, costly scheme was abandoned. What tiles had been produced were available for use in Prior Crauden's new chapel and some of the designs were adapted specially for it.

SOUTH TRANSEPT

This very worn pavement covers an area of 2.43 m by 5.08 m in the centre of the transept. The pavement is clearly relaid and it is thought that it came from the passage leading from the presbytery to the Lady chapel.[10] Like Prior Crauden's chapel pavement it is made of line-impressed mosaic. There are three panels, the centre one consisting of a large wheel about 2.20 m in diameter, with elementary trefoil decoration between sixteen rays (Fig. 7). The north panel is divided into two and is made up of an area of square tiles, occasionally inset with a small fourfoil, surrounded by small squares and rectangles, and a smaller area of similar tiles set at 45 degrees to the first. The south panel is similar to the north and south panels of the main floor of Prior Crauden's chapel.

DISCUSSION

Both the pavements belong to a large series of line-impressed mosaic pavements which spreads from Middleton Stoney, Oxfordshire, in the west, to Icklingham, Suffolk, in the east, and Helpston, Northamptonshire and King's Lynn, Norfolk, in the north.[11] The early publication of plans of Prior Crauden's chapel pavement has meant that this pavement has become the best known of the series. However, the extensive use of hand-incised decoration, not only in the Adam and Eve panel and on the lions but on the animals and birds of the small square and diamond shaped tiles, gives the pavement a place of greater importance than other material in the main series. The small square tiles with lions and stags are paralleled by

Fig. 7. S transept, roundel

similar tiles at Higham Ferrers, Northamptonshire.[12] Elizabeth Eames has written that the *sgraffito* lines around the lion and the stag were an attempt to make it look as if the animals were separate yellow tiles set in dark surrounds, like the large and small lions at Ely.[13] These large panels with small or large mosaic lions have had no parallels until recently. However, recent excavations at Old Warden, Bedfordshire, perhaps on the site of the Abbot's Lodging,[14] and Norton Priory, Cheshire[15] have produced pieces of what is clearly similar material. At Old Warden several pieces of mosaic with hand-incised decoration have been found, including a lion's face with the eyes produced in the same way as those at Ely, and a tile with *tibia* written along one side — no doubt a laying instruction for the paviour. A pavement, in many ways similar to Prior Crauden's chapel pavement has also been found in the excavations but the relationship between the two pavements and the mosaic tiles has yet to be fully investigated.

The large roundel in the south transept pavement is very simple in design compared with that at Meesden, Hertfordshire.[16] A single tile from Cambridge indicates another elaborate roundel, while another complete pavement from the monastic church at Old Warden has several elaborate roundels.[17] Small roundels occur at Helpston, Northamptonshire.[18] From present evidence, therefore, it seems that elaborate mosaic arrangements with hand-incised decoration and roundels were unusual: the majority of the surviving material in this series relies on several geometric designs with line-impressed decoration. The examination of these designs and the line-impressed stamps shows that nearly all of the known sites have enough links to suggest that, although it is not yet clear if one or several places of manufacture are involved, the same templates and stamps were used to produce tiles on a great many sites.[19]

Line-impressed mosaic tiles, however, were not confined to eastern England. An increasingly large number is found in western England and in Wales.[20] Recent work by Paul Drury has demonstrated that another type of line-impressed mosaic tile was used in Essex.[21] The use of similar patterns and stamps, clearly derived from the main Bedfordshire-Cambridgeshire-Hertfordshire-Suffolk series shows that the *Essex group* originated from this series.

The dating of the Ely pavements presents little problem. Prior Crauden's chapel pavement may be dated 1324–25 and the south transept pavement, if indeed it came from the passage leading from the presbytery to the Lady chapel, may be dated to the same period. Internal evidence at Meesden enables the pavement to be dated to the first quarter of the 14th century,[22] and the pavement at Higham Ferrers may be attributed to the remodelling of the chancel, begun in 1327.[23] It is difficult to ascertain the time range of the whole of this series but the fixed points suggest that on present evidence line-impressed mosaic pavements were unlikely to have been made much after *c.*1330.

Further work on the pavements of this series will show the full range of mosaic designs and line-impressed decoration, but it is evident, a startling archaeological discovery excepted, that Prior Crauden's chapel pavement will remain of paramount importance, not only in the series of line-impressed mosaic pavements but in the surviving medieval pavements of Britain.

ACKNOWLEDGEMENTS

I owe a special debt to Elizabeth Eames who has not only encouraged the research on line-impressed mosaic pavements but has generously discussed the material on many occasions. I am also grateful to the Rev. J. Powell, Chaplain of King's School Ely, and to Mrs Margaret Powell, for much assistance and hospitality. Mr Paul Drury has kindly discussed many points of detail, as has Mr D. W. R. Thackray whose collaboration over many years has made this preliminary study possible.

REFERENCES

1. This paper is a summary of the lecture given at the Ely conference. The descriptions and discussion are preliminary and lack full details of all the elements of the pavements. This deficiency will be rectified by an article on the tiles at Ely being prepared by the writer and Elizabeth Eames.
2. R. Gough, 'A mosaic pavement in the Prior's Chapel at Ely', *Archaeologia*, x (1792), 151–55.
3. Published 20 May 1801, as 'Principal patterns of the Roman floor in Prior Crauden's beautiful Chapel at Ely'.
4. W. Wilkins, 'An Account of the Prior's Chapel at Ely', *Archaeologia*, xiv (1803), 105–12, pl. xxviii.
5. Wilkins, op. cit., 109, records that the chapel was divided into two floors, and into two rooms with a passage, the chimney being on the north side. This conversion, which seems to have been made after the Parliamentary Commissioners' survey of 1649 when the building was valued at £33 17s., saved the building from destruction. The chapel was restored and rededicated in 1858.
6. E. S. Eames, *Medieval Tiles. A Handbook* (British Museum, London 1968), 6.
7. Wilkins's plan has these small lions facing the wrong way.
8. Chapman, i, 10, n. 5 and 64, 163.
9. F. Wormald, 'The Throne of Solomon and St Edward's Chair', in M. Meiss (ed.), *Essays in Honor of Erwin Panofsky* (New York University Press, 1961), *De Artibus Opuscula*, no. 40, 532–39. I am most grateful to Dr Pamela Tudor-Craig for this reference.
10. VCH, *Cambridge and the Isle of Ely*, iv (1953), 62a. See also C. W. Stubbs, *Handbook to the Cathedral Church of Ely*, 12th edition (Ely no date), 74.
11. See Laurence Keen, 'The Medieval Floor-tiles', in the Denny Abbey excavation report by J. G. Coad and P. M. Christie, forthcoming, for full discussion and distribution map.
12. E. S. Eames, 'The Fourteenth-century tile paving at Higham Ferrers', *Northamptonshire Past and Present*, v (1975), no. 3, 199–209.
13. Ibid., 204.
14. D. Baker, 'Bedfordshire Rescue: Round up', *Current Archaeology*, iv, no. 12 (November 1974), 369–72, and E. Baker, 'Warden Abbey, Old Warden, Beds.', in R. T. Rowley and W. J. Fowler, CBA Regional Group 9, *Newsletter*, v (1975), 22.
15. Eames, 'Higham Ferrers', 205.
16. Laurence Keen, 'A Fourteenth-century Tile Pavement at Meesden, Hertfordshire', *Hertfordshire Archaeology*, ii (1970), fig. 1 and pl. 7.
17. Plan in D. M. Wilson and D. G. Hurst, 'Medieval Britain in 1961', *Medieval Archaeology*, vi–vii (1962–63), 313 and fig. 98.
18. Laurence Keen and David Thackray, 'Helpston Parish Church, Northamptonshire: the Remains of a Medieval Tile Pavement', *JBAA*, cxxix (1976), 87–92, figs A and B.
19. A detailed discussion of this aspect must await the publication by the writer and Elizabeth Eames of a paper on the Ely pavements. Meanwhile the reader will find discussions of design and stamp links in papers on the tiles from Denny, Meesden and Helpston and in Laurence Keen and D. Thackray, 'A fourteenth-century mosaic tile pavement with line-impressed

decoration from Icklingham', *Proceedings of the Suffolk Institute of Archaeology*, XXXIII, pt 2 (1974), 153–67.
20. Elizabeth Eames and Laurence Keen, 'Some line-impressed tile mosaic from western England and Wales', *JBAA*, 3rd ser., XXXV (1972), 65–70.
21. P. Drury, 'Chelmsford Dominican Priory: The Excavation of the Reredorter, 1973', *Essex Archaeology and History*, V (1974), 71–72 and figs 14, 44, and particularly in his forthcoming report on the tiles from Rivenhall.
22. Keen, 'Meesden', 80.
23. Eames, 'Higham Ferrers', 204.

Medieval Timberwork at Ely

By JOHN FLETCHER

For medieval monastic or collegiate bodies it is fitting to consider together the roofs and other woodwork in the mother church and those in the monastic and domestic buildings around. So far there have been few accounts of the timberwork of our cathedrals and their associated buildings. Even when access to roofs is achieved, the recording *in situ* of dimensions and of the nature of the joints may not be possible, and if feasible, is invariably tedious. At Ely there is the compensation of having Atkinson's comprehensive study and the plans that accompany it, as these show what has existed at Ely and where it was or is to be found.[1] The sketch of *c*.1760 by Essex[2] when he reroofed the choir, and the sectional drawings of Bentham[3] (Pls VI and VIIA) together with early 19th-century engravings, are also helpful in revealing details now replaced or hidden.

Fortunately, Ely has not suffered the fires that make interpretation of the roofs at other cathedrals difficult and even the collapse of the central tower in 1322, although it would have damaged the roof in the east limb, left the nave roof almost unharmed.

The building of the octagon[4] and the structure of the lantern[5] have already been described but little consideration has been given to their antecedents and to answering the questions why they are unique to Ely. In contrast to the fame of the lantern, the long line of scissor-braced trusses that were erected over the nave, probably in the second quarter of the 13th century, are little known. Similar in construction to other roofing of that period at Westminster Abbey and elsewhere in England, the nave roof boldly covered a unique length of 220 ft with no longitudinal member and no tie-beam.

I do not attempt in this paper to include all the medieval woodwork that at one time or another formed part of the cathedral and related buildings at Ely. I shall first deal with problems concerning the main roofs in the cathedral and then catalogue, with reference to what has already been published, other items in the cathedral and domestic buildings. The latter, unusually, excludes the Bishop's Palace as the present building dates from the 16th century.

THE CATHEDRAL

THE NAVE

The roof now consists of twelve bays and eighty-one trusses.[6] It must be remembered, however, that when built it covered an extra bay to reach the Norman central tower. Thus no trace would survive of any damage to the first few trusses adjacent to that tower when it fell in 1322.

Stewart reasoned that the existing roof was a replacement in the time of Bishop Northwold of the Norman roof.[7] The grounds for this belief were partly its similarity to the one that had been erected over the presbytery (drawn by Essex), and partly the knowledge that Northwold had attended to the roofing at the west end of the cathedral and had added to the tower a timber spire, covered with lead. Indeed Stewart, rightly it would seem, thought it probable that Northwold roofed the church from east to west, that is, he implied new work over the whole of the east limb. The annual accounts of the time indicate that the new work was being erected between 1234 and 1252. It may be presumed that it was completed when Henry III and his court attended the dedication of the presbytery in 1252.

The date, probably in the mid or late 1230s, when the design for this roof (Fig. 1) was formulated is consistent with what we now know about the introduction of scissor-bracing and its use in England. As a form of construction it had various merits. Compared to Romanesque roofs it dispensed entirely with tie-beams and thus avoided the need for timbers of large scantling; it was suitable for the steeply-pitched roofs that were fashionable; and with lead as the covering, both for the roof itself and for the parapet walkway, rainwater could be removed without

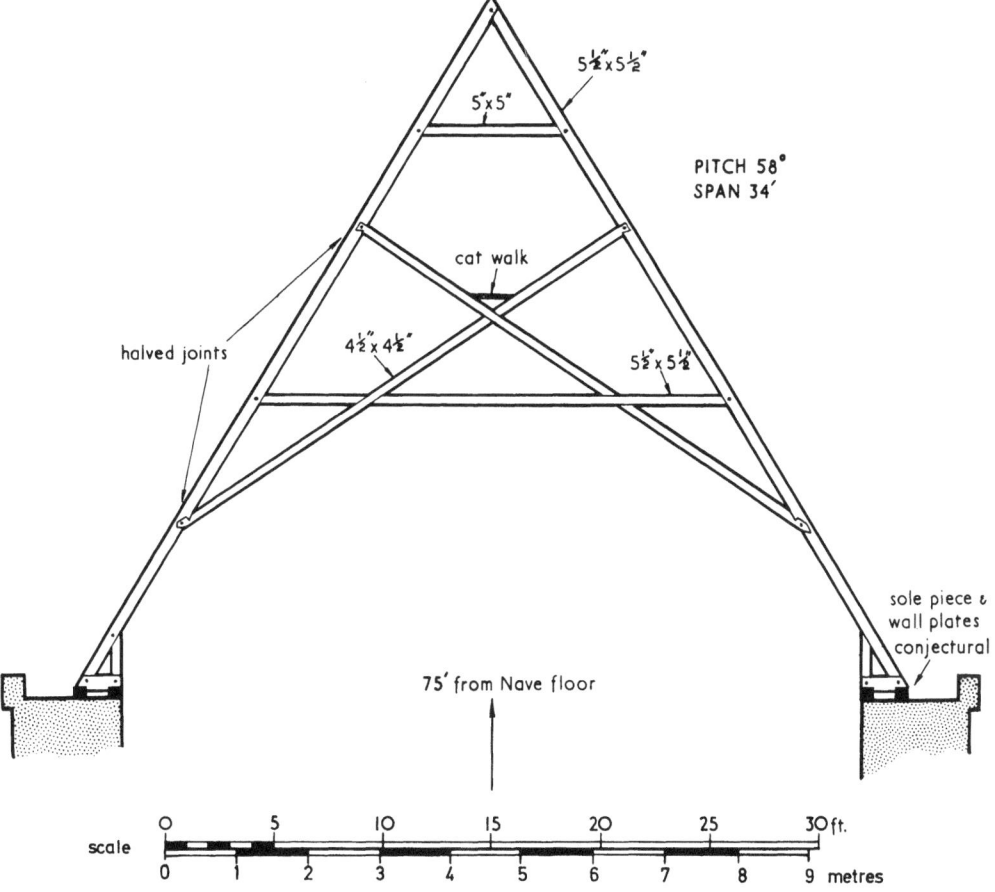

FIG. 1. Nave, section of scissor brace roof. *Author*

eaves. Furthermore, the design brought the thrust of the roof on to the centre rather than the outside of the walls.

A steeply-pitched scissor-brace roof requires oaks with long straight stems rather than trees of wide girth with low curved branches. For the Blackfriars at Gloucester, oaks from the Forest of Dean were split longitudinally to provide the long timbers required;[8] the growth of trees being less rapid in East Anglia on account of the relative dryness, whole trunks may have been used at Ely.

Isolated examples of scissor-braced roofs were indeed erected in the 14th century, but it is not correct, as some archaeologists and historians have done, to associate this system with that rather than the preceding century. As far as southern England is concerned, it was the 13th century that witnessed their introduction and their greatest use (Table 1). In the early part of that century the timbers continued to be halved to one another as in Romanesque roofs, but as the century progressed, mortice and tenon joints were used increasingly, lap joints at the feet of the scissor-braces being the last to be replaced. It was noticed by the late Donovan Purcell, when responsible for the cathedral fabric, that about half of the upper ends of the scissor-braces, namely those of the twenty-seven trusses nearest to the octagon and of twelve of the fourteen nearest to the west tower, are *halved* to the rafters (that is, have the older form of joint), while the remainder are joined by mortice and tenon.[9] The presence of halved joints strengthens the view that the nave was reroofed in Northwold's time and not later in the century.

When Essex made his examination in 1757 he found that the roof over the eastern limb (but not the nave roof) was in a bad condition as it leaned to the east

TABLE 1
Scissor-Bracing: Examples prior to A. D. 1300

	Width Spanned	Pitch	Approx. Date of Design
Tournai Cathedral, transepts	c. 30 ft	c. 53°	1190
Lincoln Cathedral, N. choir transept	8	v. steep	1195
Peterborough Cathedral, narthex*	32	52	1220
Chichester, Bishop's chapel	18	53	1220
Oxford Cathedral, chapter house	25		1225
Windsor, Henry III palace†			1225
Salisbury Cathedral, N. choir transept	25		1225
Winchester Castle, The Great Hall‡	26		1230
Ely Cathedral, presbytery and nave	34	58	1235
Westminster Abbey, transepts	36		1245
Gloucester, Blackfriars, nave and choir	27	54	1245
Harwell Church, S. transept	16	54	1280
Exeter Cathedral, presbytery	37		1290
Oxford, Merton College, choir	30	57	1290

* Reuter's suggestion that this roof had been used c.1170 in the nave has been withdrawn.
† Now in 25 The Cloisters.
‡ The present roof is a 19th-century copy.

pushing the wall out of the vertical by as much as two feet.[10] Scissor-braced roofs are prone to such canting unless effectively buttressed, at both ends, since they possess little longitudinal strengthening. It is significant that the nave roof, buttressed at both ends, by the west and central towers respectively, has not needed replacement while the roof over the eastern limb, lacking effective resistance at its eastern end, came near to collapse. Indeed the pressure exerted on the central tower as the roof to its east canted progressively may have played some part in the weakening and fall of the central tower, which, significantly, is known to have fallen to the east.

The pitch of a preceding nave roof (its slope is recorded on the east face of the west tower) had been less steep, about 50°. It would have included tie-beams and may have resembled Hewett's reconstruction of the Waltham Abbey roof.[11] Re-use of some of the earlier timbers would explain the existence in the present roof of a few beams with empty mortices for halved joints.

The nave at Ely was not alone in having no original stone vault, as the same applied at Peterborough, Norwich, Lincoln and probably Winchester. The serious damage that occurred to the walls at Lincoln late in the 12th century is believed to have arisen from the extra burden when a stone vault was added c.1140. Such experience may account for neither Peterborough nor Ely being given stone vaults, although Peterborough was boarded in the 13th century.

Ely's roof remained visible from the nave floor until boarded in the mid-19th century, as can be seen in an engraving published in 1838.[12] At that time, the open roof was regarded with conflicting views. Millers had complained in 1834 that it was 'a very great blemish' and considered it outrageous that such a magnificent nave should be covered 'with nothing more seemingly ponderous than a set of rafters scarcely stouter than those of a large parochial church or even of a substantial dwelling-house'.[13] Yet the Brandons in 1849 regarded it as the perfect example of a trussed-rafter roof, each truss when viewed from below appearing as an arch of five straight sides: they considered, probably correctly, that the span (34 feet) was the widest ever covered by this type of roof.[14]

THE OCTAGONAL LANTERN AND ITS SUPPORTING FRAME

It was a bold decision, after the fall of the central tower in 1322, to enlarge the open space to a width of 70 ft to be vaulted in wood and crowned by a lantern (Plate VIIb). It remained the largest open central area in an English cathedral until that formed under Wren's dome at St Paul's and it is of interest to note that Brunelleschi's masterpiece at Florence was a century later than the octagon at Ely.

In 1322, polygonal forms in church architecture were fashionable and piers and timber posts of octagonal section for arcades and crown-posts respectively were commonplace. The technique of dispensing with a proportion of the tie-beams in the earlier Romanesque roofs, where there was one to each truss, had emerged in Flanders and Hainault by the middle of the 12th century (Fig. 2).[15] Triangulation by relatively long sole-pieces and ashlars, eventually used on a larger scale in hammerbeam roofs, was the principle employed. Scissor-braced roofing carried

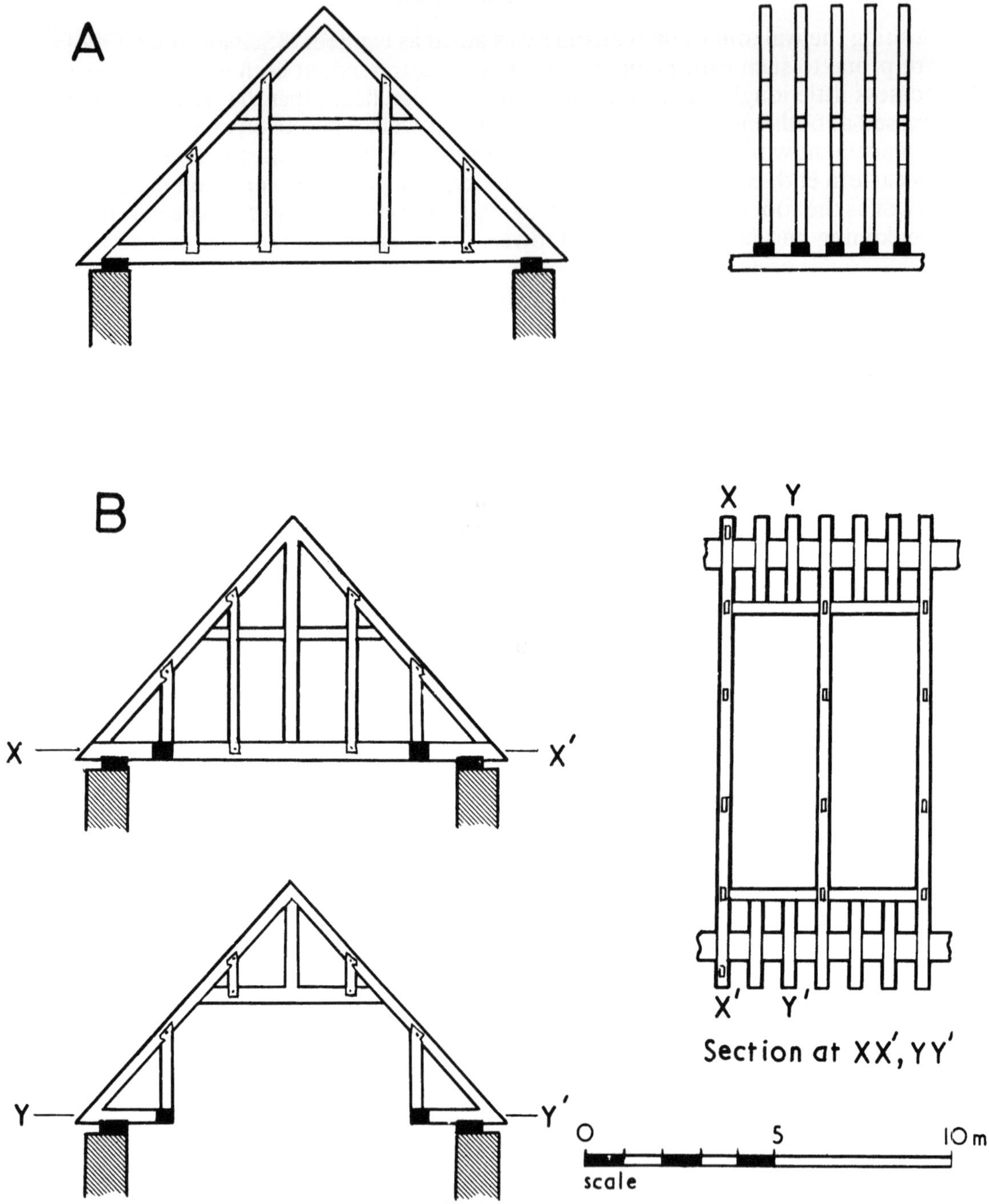

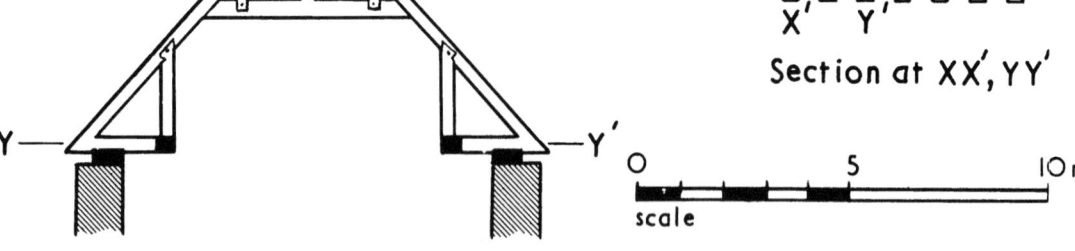

Fig. 2. Soignies Abbey, Romanesque roofs
(A) Nave, eleventh century. Note the tie beam at each truss
(B) Choir, mid-twelfth century. *Above*: the tie beam truss, only present with every third pair of rafters. *Below*: the 'hammerbeam' truss derived by eliminating the centre of the tie beam. (After S. Brigode, *Bull. Commission royale des Monuments et des Sites*, I (1949))

the elimination of tie-beams a stage further, leaving an open structure as high as the collars. The novelty of the octagon at Ely was partly that the openness achieved was not linear as in a nave, but at a crossing: partly in the size of the area spanned, 70 ft, within which was a central void, 30 ft across, formed by an octagonal 'ring' of horizontal beams. It is possible that the scheme, made feasible by creating a void that was octagonal, occurred to the master craftsmen concerned because they were conditioned at that time to the general use of this form in other contexts. Had the central tower fallen a generation earlier or a generation later, the outcome might well have been different.

In terms of covering a large area with no central support, the Ely octagon and lantern represent a leap forward, but there were precedents in England in the previous half-century on a smaller scale. In one, the roof over the square kitchen (34 ft × 34 ft) of the Bishop's Palace at Chichester, the framing leaves a central void 18 ft square by using the hammerbeam principle.[16] In May 1978, Julian Munby and I came to the conclusion, by comparing it with the 13th-century roofs of St Mary's Hospital, the nearby chapel of the Bishop's Palace and of the cathedral itself, that this kitchen was roofed c. 1300 or shortly before.[17]

A different precedent for the Ely lantern was the chapter house at York, built in the last years of the 13th century.[18] Large polygonal chapter houses of earlier date, such as that at Westminster, had included a central shaft, but the roof at York covered a span of 59 feet with no such support. Its design, a central king-post on tie-beams at right-angles, was out of the question for the octagon at Ely where an open space for the lantern was required. In both roofs the timbers were steeply-pitched (60°) to cope with the large thrusts involved, for the lantern at Ely weighs more than 450 tons. York had the nearby Forest of Galtres to supply oak beams over 50 ft long (the king-post measures 64 feet). At Ely, however, there were no local oaks for the longest baulks and so provision of suitable timber involved long and perhaps difficult journeys.

Atkinson argues in his description in the *Victoria County History* that although the stonework may have been ready for the timber structure in 1328, there followed a pause and the latter was not erected until 1334-37 when William Hurley himself was resident at Ely.[19] Reference has often been made to the £9 paid to Chicksands Priory in 1322-23 for 20 oaks which were felled and brought to Ely, a distance of about 40 miles, the next year. The demand at that time, however, was for scaffolding and it is only conjectural that these trees formed part of the timbers erected some twelve years later for the lantern. The Sacrist Rolls show that purchases of timber at the markets of Barnwell, Stourbridge, Hilgay and Reach continued over the years. The scarf joints noticed by Hewett on some of the longest timbers imply that insufficient single trunks existed to meet the requirements for the longest members.[20]

The design of the original timber-framing, with the additions by Essex excluded, has been deduced and illustrated by Hewett (Fig. 3). Basically there had to be two stages: the first, the cobweb of ribs springing from the stone octagon together with the perforated platform around the octagonal void (Fig. 3a); the second (Fig. 3b), the insertion of the vertical posts of the lantern on to that platform and their

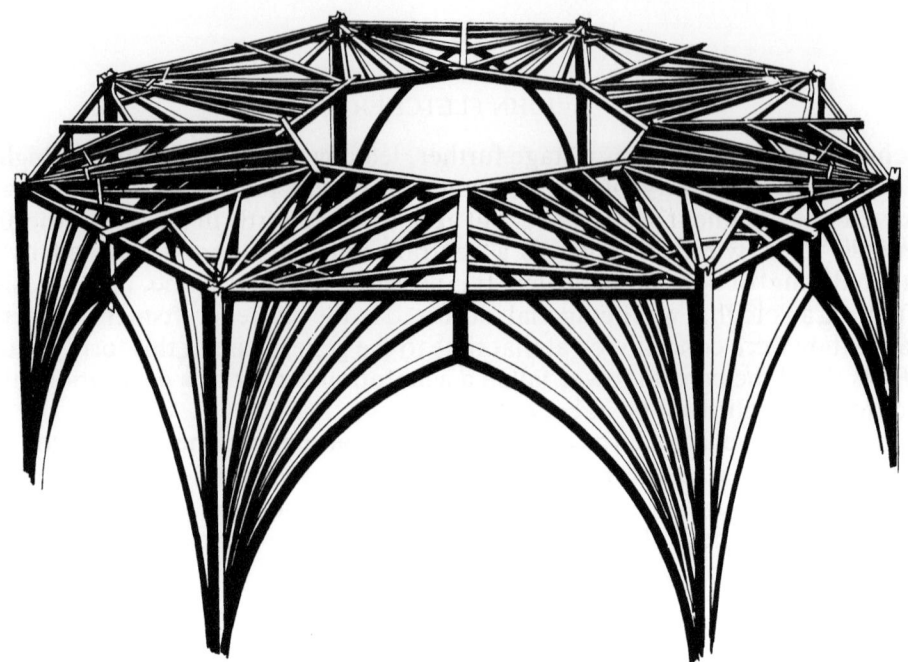

(A) Framework over the octagon forming a perforated, platform around the central octagonal void

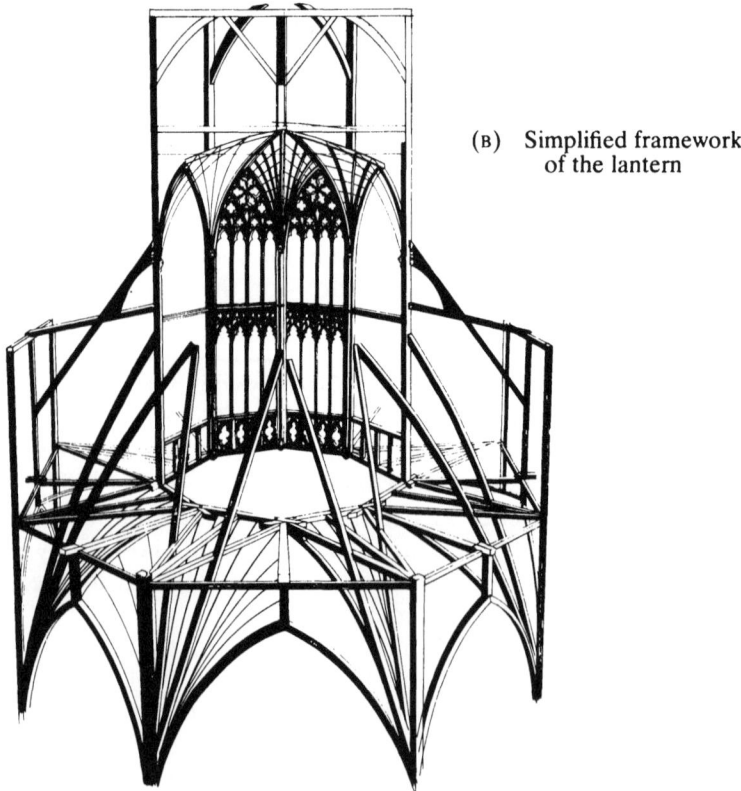

(B) Simplified framework of the lantern

FIG. 3. Construction of the Octagon (Hewett, *English Cathedral Carpentry* (1974), figs 75 and 76)

stabilisation by long, steeply-inclined shores that were set into grooves in the stonework. The accounts mention the purchase of Rigold boards (that is, from the port of Riga on the Baltic) in 1323–24 and of Estrich boards (imported via Lynn) in 1334–35. Such boards would have been used between the ribs of the octagon's vault and for the lowest section of the lantern (Plate VIIB). Presumably they survive, like the imported boarding of fir used in a partition at Westminster Abbey in the time of Richard II.[21]

The ravages of beetle attack led Gilbert Scott to add constructional timbers and to strengthen the trusses which hold up the lantern. Further repairs, together with protection of the timber, were carried out soon after the Appeal of 1951, by which time Scott's new woodwork had itself been attacked.[22]

CENTRAL TRANSEPTS

These were given hammerbeam roofs in the 15th century.[23]

GALILEE

The doors have been described and illustrated by Hewett, who points out they are the only example of the counter-rebated type to have survived in England.[24] Believing that the porch was added c.1250, he suggested they were reused after being designed in the late 12th century. It seems more likely, as a date of c.1215 is now usually accepted for the porch, that they are original work of that date.

STALLS AND MISERICORDS

Originally placed in the octagon, these were carved and constructed c.1340, probably to designs by William Hurley who was receiving payments at Ely at that time.[25]

MONASTIC AND OTHER DOMESTIC BUILDINGS

The dominant role in the local community that the Bishop of Ely continued to play until limited by an Act of 1836 (the powers and rights of the Liberty of Ely approached those of a County Palatine) aided the preservation of various medieval buildings that would doubtless have been swept aside in an expanding commercial city (Pl. I). Thus the large aisled barn that was built near the Green in the mid-13th century for the sacrist was not demolished until 1842. From the description and drawings made by Willis just before its demolition, it appears to have retained its original timber roof (still thatched over the nave) and thereby adds substantially to our knowledge of aisled barns at that time.[26]

Similarly, some 12th-century roofing, a rarity in England, has survived at Ely as at Peterborough.[27] The examples in both cities confirm the view that Romanesque roofing of stone ranges in eastern England was similar to contemporary Romanesque timberwork on the continent. In the succeeding centuries, the use of straight rather than curved timber continued to dominate timber-framing at Ely, as elsewhere in eastern England. Thus the use of elbowed beams as short principles (so-called base-crucks) that was adopted for halls in the south midlands and further west from c.1300 onwards is absent at Ely. In the section that follows, surviving or known medieval work is listed in chronological order.

THE WEST RANGE

An eight-bay range, originally the cellarer's, was added to the prior's group of buildings towards the end of the 12th century. The original roof survives for seventeen trusses (about 40 ft) from the north wall.[28] The rafters, collars and struts, all of Romanesque form are held together by halved joints. Raising of the walls in the 13th century led to the elimination of the tie-beams that were probably present at every fifth truss. However, their ends, originally resting *on* the walls, appear to survive on the east side *in* the raised wall.

THE SEXTRY BARN

This barn, already mentioned above, was a stone building of eleven bays almost 220 ft long with an internal width of 40 ft. Willis's drawing (Fig. 4) shows that the oak posts of the nave would have been 22 ft high, and the passing braces or secondary rafters that run parallel to the main rafters 36 ft long.

THE GREAT HALL

This high building (now the bishop's house), 80 ft × 30 ft in size and of five bays, has undergone various changes and been the subject of much study.[29] Many distinguished visitors would have been entertained in it. The building dates from the first half of the 13th century and my own investigation in 1965 indicated that the two bays at the west end, separated in the undercroft by a stone wall, have the original roofing. Each truss is seven-sided and is like the nave roof, except for the absence of the upper (scissor) part of the bracing. The beams are smoke-blackened.

During the early 14th-century reconstruction, the roof of the hall, always at first-floor level, was modified below the collars to its present form. There are short uncurved principals and arch-braces tenoned into internal wall posts that rest on corbels carved with figures (Fig. 5). It forms an East Anglian counterpart to the contemporary halls with short, elbowed, principals that were built, for example, in North Berkshire and the West Midlands.

THE BLACK HOSTRY

Chronologically, the timberwork of this building (Fig. 5) datable from the accounts to 1291–92, falls between the two phases represented in the Great Hall. It is of five bays, with first-floor walls of stone on the north and timber on its south side and was used for the accommodation of visiting monks. Its crown-post and collar purlin roof — the only one that survives at Ely — has octagonal posts and in the partition truss there are downward braces.

THE PRIOR'S HALL

This hall, over a Romanesque undercroft, was rebuilt in the 14th century and given a 'curb' or mansard roof. Atkinson pointed out that this truncated form of roof was peculiar to the eastern parts of England and recorded other examples of the same period over the main transepts and at the west end of the cathedral.

SOUTHERN EXTENSION OF THE WEST RANGE

The extension of c.1360 of five bays on a brick undercroft retains its original roofing, which includes side purlins.

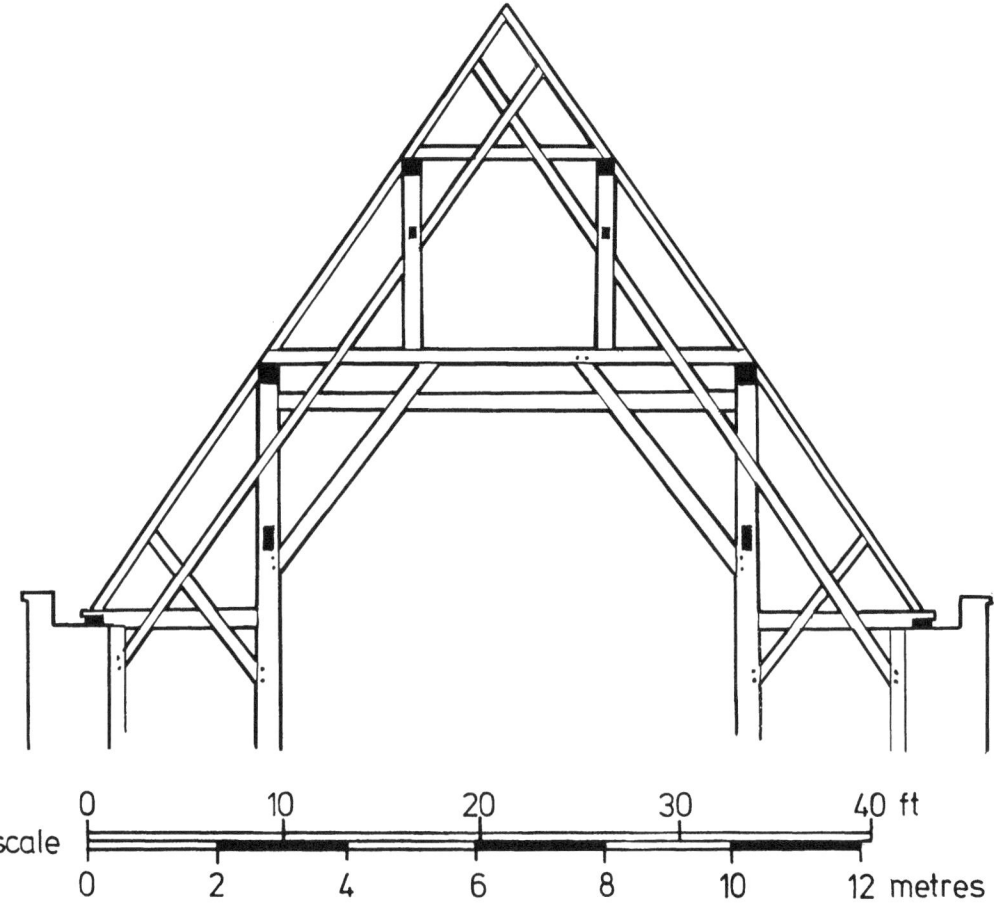

FIG. 4. Sextry barn, section, mid-thirteenth century (after Willis, op. cit., note 26)

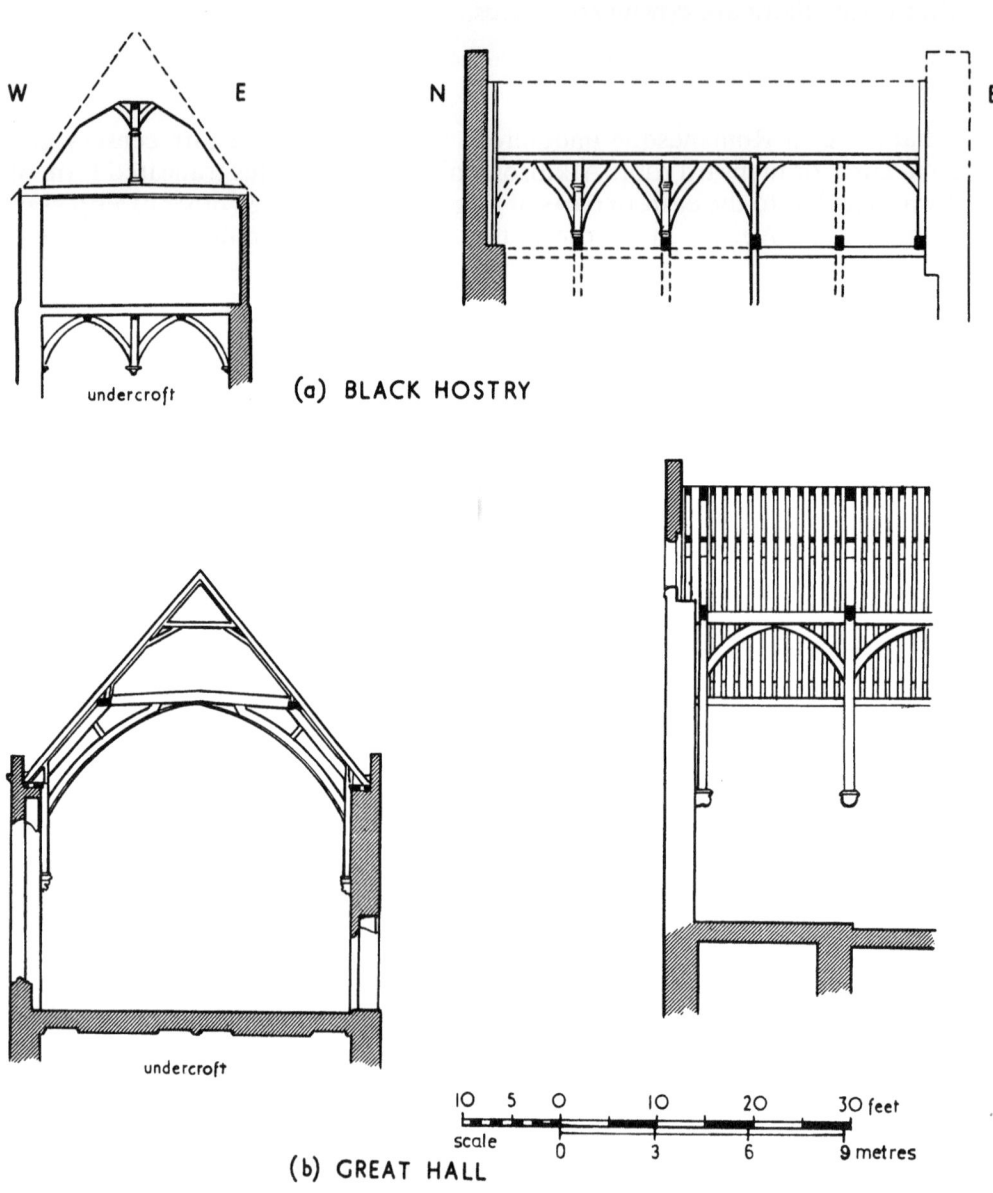

FIG. 5. (from Atkinson, 1933)

(A) Black Hostry, section (B) Great Hall, section

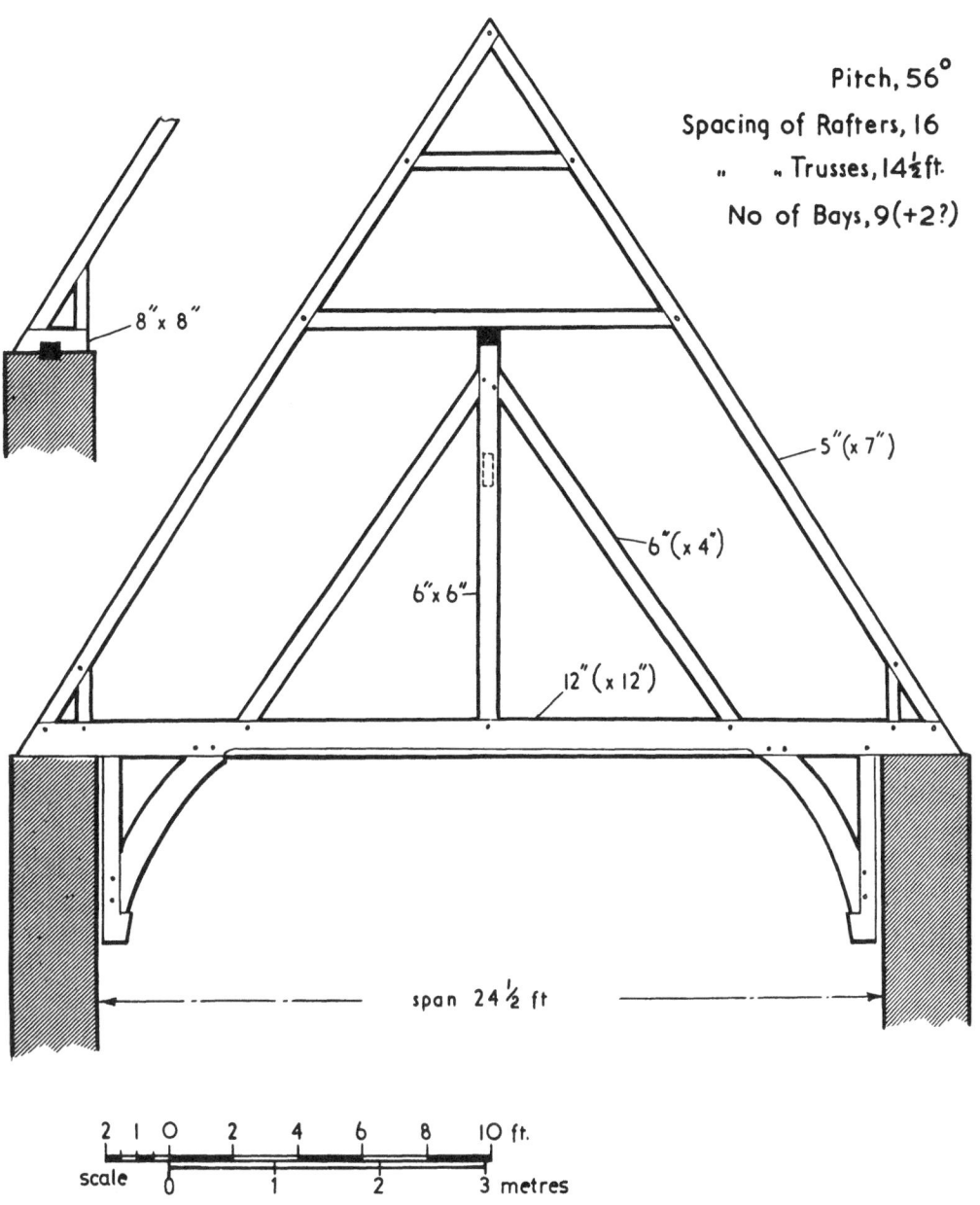

FIG. 6. Barn near Ely Porta, section of roof, c.1400. *Author*

BARN

The long stone barn near the Porta now forms the King's School dining-room at first-floor level. It has an open timber roof with tie-beams between its ten bays (Fig. 6). Atkinson proposed a date of c.1375, but there seems little evidence for it being earlier than 1400, the date at which the nearby Ely Porta was in course of erection.

ACKNOWLEDGEMENTS

I am grateful to present and past Deans of Ely who have permitted me to have access to the cathedral roofs; to the occupants of houses in the close vicinity who have allowed me to inspect medieval roofs; to the staff of the King's School for access to their buildings and for information; and to colleagues who have helped with measurements and participated in discussions. I wish to thank Mr Cecil Hewett for kindly allowing me to reproduce from his book, *English Cathedral Carpentry*, the drawings that form Fig. 3.

REFERENCES

1. Atkinson, 1933.
2. B.L. Add. MS 6772, f. 221.
3. Bentham, 1771.
4. VCH, *Cambridge and the Isle of Ely*, IV (1953), 62–65.
5. C. A. Hewett, *English Cathedral Carpentry* (London 1974), 82–89.
6. J. M. Fletcher and P. S. Spokes, 'The Origin and Development of Crown-Post Roofs', *Medieval Archaeology*, VIII (1964), 160–62.
7. Stewart, 43, 75.
8. O. Rackham, W. J. Blair and J. T. Munby, 'The Thirteenth Century Roofs and Floor of the Blackfriars Priory at Gloucester', *Medieval Archaeology*, XXII (1978), 105–22.
9. Private Communication, 11 August 1965.
10. 1757. Report to Dean and Chapter of Ely; B.L. Add. MS. 6769.
11. C. A. Hewett, op. cit., Fig. 2, page 16.
12. R. Garland in B. Winkles, *Cathedral Churches of England and Wales*, II (1838), Pl. 71.
13. G. Millers, *Ely Cathedral* (1834).
14. R. and J. A. Brandon, *Open Roofs of the Middle Ages* (1849).
15. Fletcher and Spokes, op. cit., 156–57.
16. VCH., *Sussex*, III (1935), 151; *Archaeol. J.*, XCII (1935), 390.
17. J. Munby in *Chichester Excavations*, **4**, ed. A. Down (Phillimore, forthcoming).
18. J. Q. Hughes, 'The Timber Roofs of York Minster', *Yorkshire Archaeological Journal*, 38 (1955), 474–95; and Hewett, op. cit., 74–76.
19. VCH, *Cambridge and the Isle of Ely*, IV (1953), 64.
20. Hewett, op. cit., 89.
21. J. M. Fletcher, unpublished observation.
22. S. E. Dykes Bower, 'The Architect Explains', Appeals Pamphlet, 1951, 4.
23. Illustrated as Frontispiece to Hewett, op. cit.
24. Ibid., Fig. 85.
25. VCH, *Cambridge and the Isle of Ely*, IV (1953), 64.
26. R. Willis, 'A Description of the Sextry Barn at Ely lately Demolished', *Proceedings of the Cambridge Antiquarian Society*, I (1843), Item 6.
27. J. M. Fletcher and R. Taylor, 'A Norman Hall with its Original Roof', *Friends of Peterborough Cathedral*, 1972, 7–9.
28. J. M. Fletcher and W. F. O. Haslop, 'The West Range at Ely and its Romanesque Roof', *Archaeol. J.*, CXXVI (1969), 171–76.
29. P. A. Faulkner, 'Ely: The Monastic Buildings South of the Cloister', *Archaeol. J.*, CXXIV (1967), 216–21.

The Architectural History of Ely Cathedral from 1540–1840

By THOMAS COCKE

The architectural history of Ely cathedral from the Dissolution to the reign of Queen Victoria is worthy of study on two counts. Firstly, the medievalist must discover whether the structures he is examining have been affected by this period as well as by the more notorious 19th century. Secondly, the work done not only possesses its own intrinsic interest and value, it also reveals the attitudes of contemporaries towards the great medieval monuments which Time had left stranded in their midst, in defiance of prevailing standards of convenience and taste. This paper leaves off the story with the arrival of Tractarian and Puginian dedication in the field of church restoration, since the earlier period, quite apart from being much less known, has to be understood according to financial, ecclesiastical and aesthetic criteria quite different from those of the past 150 years.

The first major event in the post-Reformation history of Ely cathedral occurred in 1566 when the Lady chapel was assigned as the Trinity parish church in the place of the 14th–15th-century church which stood just north of the nave.[1] The church probably abutted directly on the cathedral wall as a 'lean-to' rather than standing apart with a communicating passage, since, when its remains were finally tidied away in 1662, the north aisle had to be recased.[2] The door opening to it from the cathedral survives behind Bishop Woodford's monument. The change in parish church was not all loss, since it ensured the survival and proper maintenance of the dangerously isolated Lady chapel, whose only major loss was the smashing of the sculptured groups in the arcading. Although Ely, being such a staunchly Parliamentarian area, must have suffered from the renewed Puritan onslaught on 'graven images' which accompanied the Civil Wars, there is no evidence to ascribe this particularly brutal act of iconoclasm to the mid-17th century, let alone to William Dowsing himself.[3] Paradoxically, traces of the original painting of the sculptures survived until the major repair and refurbishing of the building in 1806. The cathedral itself was at risk during the Civil War period. In 1647–48 there was a scheme to demolish it entirely and sell its materials for the benefit of 'sick and maimed soldiers, Widows and Orphans'.[4] Many of the conventual buildings did disappear in the 1650s although the Parliamentary survey of 1650 preparatory to their sale preserves some record of them. The chapter house and most of the cloister vanished, causing the Chapter after the Restoration to meet in a chapel in the south transept. The south-west corner of the transept seems to have suffered from the removal of the abutting cloister, so in 1696–98 it was given a massive buttress by Robert Grumbold the leading Cambridge mason (Pl. XIXB). This was pierced by a simple but well-designed rusticated door so that, together with the remains of the cloister, a sort of vestibule to the church was formed.

In the years immediately following the Restoration much money had to be spent on the cathedral. Loans as much as £1,000 were raised from individual members of the Chapter. The only obvious surviving work of the period is the recasing of the north aisle in 1662, recorded on a date stone on the exterior, although in 1669 the west tower was repaired in order to receive the bells from the lantern. Bishop Gunning (1628–84) deployed most of his generosity on the episcopal residences but he did re-pave the choir, thus starting several of the medieval monuments on their ever more fragile course about the church. He is also supposed to have been the first to project moving the choir eastward.

The tranquillity of the precinct was rudely disturbed when the north-west corner of the north transept collapsed about 10 p.m. on 29 March 1699, whether because of an earthquake some years earlier (the dean's theory) or because of defects in the pier at the north-west angle (Wren's) (Pl. XVIIIb). The supervision of the restoration was entrusted to the best authorities, that is, the Royal Works establishment of Wren, Bankes the Master Carpenter and ffulkes, the overseer of the masons' work at St Paul's. Repair was carried out swiftly and to a high standard. Robert Grumbold of Cambridge who had built the buttress on the south front and who, through his work at Trinity College, had direct experience of Christopher Wren's work, carried out the actual rebuilding. Its extent outside is easily distinguished since the later work is in a lighter coloured stone, but it is hard to determine how much was affected inside, particularly in the north gallery.

It is significant that such a high standard of repair was required for a superfluous part of the cathedral. The north transept was in practical terms simply a vast entrance hall: with the choir still closed off in the crossing it could not even be used for extra seating at special services. The letters by Dean Lambe[5] about the restoration appear to show that he was principally concerned he might have to put his hand too deeply in his own pocket, but they also show that he consulted Sir Christopher Wren and Samuel ffulkes closely, rather as the Oxford authorities consulted Wren about the possible collapse of the Divinity School at this time.[6] Bishop Patrick had Court and London connections through his successive preferments at St Paul's, Covent Garden, Westminster Abbey and elsewhere, and through his literary achievements, and he may have influenced the decision to make the restoration a proper job, not a provincial patch-up. Archbishop Tenison was interested in the work, telling the Dean to consult with Wren 'or other builders' and report back to him.

The work is exemplary for its care, amply fulfilling the Chapter's order that the transept was to be rebuilt 'exactly in ye same manner and on ye same foundations it stood before'.[7] The Romanesque mouldings are reproduced faithfully although the 18th-century stonework has a crispness of cut unknown to the 12th century. The bases of the columns in the triforium inevitably reveal a knowledge of classical Tuscan models: the grotesques of the north-west 'tourelle' are rendered in a vigorous contemporary translation of those on the surviving original (Pls XVId and f). The pinnacle on the north-west corner of the aisle is copied from the elaborate 14th-century ones on the flying buttresses to the octagon, which seems unlikely to have been the case before (Pl. XVIe).

The only place where a contemporary touch was introduced was at the western end of the transept's north wall. There a great Romanesque-type window with recessed orders was given, like the windows of Trinity College library, Cambridge, two mullions and a transom while the portal beneath was adapted from that at the base of Wren's tower to St Mary le Bow in the City of London (itself derived from Mansart's Hotel de Conti) (Pl. XVIIIB). The door has been the target of much abuse — Buckler deliberately left it out of his print of the north transept — but it does respect the general character of the Romanesque work, with its round head and recessed orders. Could it be, like Inigo Jones's nave at Old St Paul's, a case of Tuscan being thought the proper contemporary equivalent to Romanesque?[8] It certainly seems to be much grander than its predecessor as somewhat murkily shown in King's print in the *Monasticon*.[9] The Dean and Chapter had their door on the south, the bishop his gallery from the Palace to the west; perhaps this was to be the tardy answer for the townspeople on the north side.

The presiding genius of Ely's architectural history in the 18th century was no artist or prelate but an antiquary, James Bentham. Bentham spent nearly all his long life in Ely acquiring first a minor canonry and then a prebend, not to mention various parish livings in which he never resided. He was clearly not one of the liveliest minds of the century, even if we discount the waspish remark by William Cole that Bentham was a 'most forcible instance of ignorance and obstinacy being coupled together'.[10] His *magnum opus*, *The History and Antiquities of the Conventual and Cathedral Church of Ely from 673 to 1771* is, however, one of the finest cathedral histories ever written, with its massive and careful accumulation of facts, and its high standard of illustration. The brief history of pre-Renaissance English architecture with which the book is prefaced, was easily the most ambitious yet to have been attempted. Thomas Gray, although he did not, as was sometimes claimed, virtually write it,[11] made valuable criticisms of Bentham's draft and contributed a perceptive analysis of Romanesque mouldings. The characterisations of the succeeding architectural periods, if not always right, are shrewd and show a deep knowledge of the contemporary literary sources, from Bede onwards.

Bentham was a doer as well as a writer. Besides interesting himself in draining the fens or making turnpikes, he engaged in practical preservation, such as in rescuing Ovin's stone from its lowly use as a horse block at Haddenham and scraping the whitewash from the sculptures on Bishop West's tomb. When the mid-century restoration was begun under James Essex, Bentham acted in effect as clerk of the works and, in particular, campaigned for and superintended the controversial removal of the choir.

The immediate impetus for this restoration seems to have been given by the aged Bishop Mawson, who gave very generously to the rebuilding and 'beautifying' of the east end of the cathedral, requiring that his donation should be matched by the Dean and Chapter.[12] It is probably the combination of James Bentham, Bishop Mawson and, most important, James Essex the architect, which ensured that the restoration of the cathedral carried out from 1757–71 was thorough yet scholarly, unlike the hopeful patching tried so disastrously at Hereford cathedral in these years.

James Essex was just at the beginning of his career as a Gothicist. He had been educated literally in the shadow of King's College chapel which had fired him with an admiration for medieval architecture, but until his Ely work he had chiefly been engaged as a coadjutor of Sir William Burrough, the amateur architectural panjandrum of Augustan Cambridge, in classical refashionings of various colleges. It is not clear whether the Dean and Chapter already knew Essex's medieval interests when they invited him to survey the cathedral in 1757 or whether they simply asked him because, like Grumbold sixty years before, he was the leading architect in Cambridge.

According to Pevsner, Essex 'began work in 1757 and did not, on the whole, do much'.[13] It is, rather, the case that very little now visible has survived the attentions of G. G. Scott a century later.[14] Essex's survey of 1757 showed that much was wrong with the building. The lead and timbers of the roof were in a very bad state, particularly at the east end over the presbytery, where, moreover, the timbers had forced the east wall (supposedly weakened in the early 16th century by the insertion of the West and Alcock chapels) two feet out of true. The lantern was threatening collapse with only half of its sixteen 'great timbers' intact.[15] Lead had been added to the roof in order to prevent more wet coming in but its weight had merely compounded the problems.

Essex firmly told the Dean and Chapter that a 'partial repair' would be 'the greatest Imprudence and Extravagance', especially since 'neglect of the lantern would lead to the Destruction of the Church'.[16] It was probably to ensure that these vital repairs were not economised upon, that Essex was prepared to condemn the Galilee and the south-west transept as neither ornamental nor useful, and to recommend that their materials could be better used elsewhere.[17] Neither was an integral part of the cathedral — the south-west transept, crazily patched up, served as the cathedral workshop until the 1840s — and would therefore lack a practical let alone aesthetic reason for preservation. Essex was, however, directed to repair the Galilee in 1762.

It is surprisingly hard to describe Essex's repairs in detail. The late 1750s saw an immediate start on the most urgent tasks. The first of these was to restore the east end (Pl. XIXA). Probably only the upper parts of the wall were dismantled and rebuilt, although a later source states that the wall was screwed back to the perpendicular as had been done for the 1719 repair of the Beverley north transept.[18] The roofing over the whole of the eastern part of the church was renewed to Essex's design.[19] The octagon was rebuilt in the late 1750s, with the rotten timbers replaced within, the openings filled with simple Y tracery and the angles crowned with modest pinnacles (frontispiece). It looks rather Gothick beside Scott's beefy Victorian version but it is closer to the appearance of its predecessor, as shown in the engravings in the *Monasticon* and Browne Willis. There is no evidence that Scott had more authority for his reconstruction than Essex.[20]

The mundane work of repairing stone, wood and lead is even harder to trace.[21] Essex was very anxious to have this type of repair done properly. He hated the improvidence with which previous workmen had inserted iron ties or wooden struts to cobble together decayed parts of the fabric instead of affording new sections. Concerning previous efforts to repair the east end, he commented that 'nothing was done as it ought to have been though the Expense [of former attempts] was as great if not greater' than a proper repair would have cost.[22] The best summary of all this type of work was given by the Rev. D. J. Stewart in 1868: 'In executing repairs absolutely essential to the safety of the building, Mr Essex showed great professional skill and unusual respect for the workmanship of an earlier period. He took all possible pains to save every fragment of old timber that could be kept in its original place, and can claim the credit of having carried out his work in a purely conservative spirit.'[23]

The aspect of Essex's restoration which dominated all others to the minds of contemporaries, was the removal of the choir from the middle of the church to the far east end. It was first projected in 1757–59 but it was not executed until 1770–71, because of a shortage of funds (Pl. IV).[24] The choir had been laid out in the original church on the usual late 11th-century plan, embracing the crossing and a few bays of the nave, with a stone pulpitum closing it off to the west (Pl. III). This arrangement lost its logic at the Reformation when the destruction of the shrine of St Etheldreda left the area to the east of the presbytery empty and functionless. What more natural than that the choir, instead of cluttering up the middle of the building, where sound and heat were lost to the lantern, should be moved to the presbytery on which so much money had just been spent in repairs? So ran the practical argument, with which was coupled the aesthetic argument that a clear vista would thus be obtained through the building.

The major archaeological loss caused by the removing of the choir was the destruction of the 12th-century pulpitum. Perhaps revealingly, Bentham does not even mention it in his book. Essex did at least sketch some of its details and is said to have re-used parts in his own screen.[25]

In the new choir the altar was placed under the east window and the organ over a gallery at its west end.[26] The medieval stalls, carefully repaired, provided the model for the Gothic detailing of the whole work which, like Essex's similar work at the east end of King's chapel Cambridge later in the decade, set new standards of authenticity.[27] It is instructive to compare Essex's treatment of the choir with that of Scott, who moved it again though not back to its traditional place, adding a screen in no way corresponding to the Romanesque original and inserting extraneous terracotta reliefs into the upper canopies of the stalls.

The moving of the choir caused further damage to the surviving medieval tombs. Several of those moved by Bishop Gunning were displaced again, while the Cardinal of Luxembourg's tomb, being too big to move, was boarded up to accommodate the new reredos. Bishop Hotham's monument was split up, with the canopy going into the north choir arcade and the tomb into the south.[28] Both Bentham and Cole were strangely insensitive to this 'general post'.[29]

The areas least touched by Essex's restoration were the west tower and transept and the Galilee, although in his survey he emphasised the dangerous lack of bonding between the 12th-century tower and its 14th-century octagonal top; presumably the funds ran out. In 1796 the Chapter called in James Wyatt to do a survey of the cathedral, concentrating on the western parts. The mildness of his report belies his reputation as a cathedral wrecker. What exactly he intended for the ruined northern transept and the ruinous southern is obscure: basically they were to be left until there could be a proper rebuilding campaign at the west end. He also recommended raising the bell stage so that a clear view could be obtained into 'a very beautiful part of the Saxon tower rich in columns and Arches clearly intended to be seen'.[30] Some of the work he recommended was carried out in 1802, when extensive repairs were made to the west tower. At the same time, considerable work was done on the Galilee, at the instigation of Bishop Yorke. The roof was lowered so that the west window, to which the bishop gave some medieval Flemish glass, could be seen from the nave. The portal itself had its mouldings 'curiously restored to their original beauty and finish' by an artificial composition stone. Inside a different and less successful type of plaster was used. The smaller doors which had been inserted in the entrance arches, probably, to judge from the *Monasticon* print, even before the Dissolution, were removed. Bernasconi (who perhaps owed his employment to the new medium used) refashioned the tympana of the inner and outer portals. The latter remains unaltered by Scott.

Apart from a further tidying-up of the Galilee by the bishop in 1807 and the 1806 repairs to the Lady chapel, mentioned at the beginning, there is little but a new organ to record before the great Victorian restoration campaigns started in the 1840s. The transition was marked by a strangely fitting catastrophe in 1845 when George Basevi, one of the most enthusiastically Renaissance architects of the 19th century, fell to his death when incautiously investigating Ely's medieval roofs.

REFERENCES

1. The church was originally dedicated to the Holy Cross but it had been transferred to the Trinity before the Dissolution.
2. Dr D. Owen, Curator in Ecclesiastical Archives at Cambridge University Library, confirms this suggestion.
3. Although Dowsing had a commission from the Earl of Manchester to visit the churches of the Associated Counties (which included the County and University of Cambridge as well as Suffolk), there is no evidence that his activities extended to the Isle of Ely. The Rev. C. H. Evelyn White, ed., *Journal of William Dowsing* (Ipswich 1885), 17.
4. B.L. Add. MS 5868, f. 34v. (Cole), f. 37 (BM).
5. Ely Diocesan Archives on deposit at Cambridge University Library 4/5, published in P. Moore, *Three Restorations of Ely Cathedral* (Ely 1973), 3–6. The minor canon John Dowsing, who acted as treasurer for the repair fund, made a formal note that 'no dangerous Cracks nor warnings of this Ruin were observed before it happened . . . and here it may be recorded to ye honour of this Society that all first appearances of decay in this noble edifice have been always timely obviated by ye extraordinary care and zeal of the Chapter: of this I have been a witness for two and twenty years'. Ely Diocesan Archives 4/6/8.
6. Bodl. MS 907.
7. Chapter Act Book, Ely Diocesan Archives, 2/1/1.
8. J. Summerson, *Inigo Jones* (London 1966), 103.
9. William Dugdale, *Monasticon* (London 1655), plate opp. p. 88.

10. W. Stevenson, *Supplement and Notes to Bentham's Ely* (Norwich 1817), 4.
11. Ibid., 12–17.
12. P. Moore, op. cit., 9–10. Bishop Mawson's rebuilding of the town jail, which is held up as laughable by Canon Moore, showed that the bishop had a welcome sense of responsibility about his judicial duties as a palatine magistrate.
13. B/E, *Cambridgeshire*, 2nd ed. (London 1970), 342.
14. Scott rebuilt the octagon and moved the choir yet again, in both cases destroying Essex's work completely.
15. B.L. Add. MS 6769. See also C. Hewett, *English Cathedral Carpentry* (London 1971), 85.
16. B.L. Add. MS 6769, ff. 155–56.
17. Ibid., f. 172.
18. G. Millers, *Description of the Cathedral Church of Ely* (Ely 1807), 74. Essex also replaced the Lady chapel roof in 1762.
19. Bentham, 284.
20. Stewart, 127.
21. For his contemporary work on the roofs see Hewett, op. cit., 130.
22. B.L. Add. MS 6769, f. 159.
23. Stewart 127.
24. A forceful letter by Essex in favour of the move survives, dated 1759. In it he refers to criticism of the scheme by an 'Eminent Architect' (so far unidentified), B.L. Add. MS 5842, 352.
25. In 'Quire Screens in English Cathedrals . . .', *Archaeologia*, LXVIII (1917), 43–110, W. St J. Hope published a reconstruction of the screen, reproducing some of Essex's engravings. Essex's brief description of it was published in W. Stevenson, op. cit., Addenda, 3.
26. Essex himself had wanted the organ on the east wall as an 'Elegant Termination' of the view down the church, on the model of the Royal Chapel at Versailles. D. R. Stewart, 'James Essex', *Architectural Review*, 108 (1950), 318, and B.L. Add. MS 5843, 15. Horace Walpole was mobilised by Cole to support the scheme but conservatism must have won the day. H. Walpole, *Correspondence*, I, ed. W. S. Lewis (London 1937), 185.
27. The VCH, though fair to Essex's restoration, strangely claims the reredos of the new choir was classical, VCH, *Cambridge and the Isle of Ely*, IV, 75. The only detailed view of the choir as built is in Winkles' *Cathedrals*, II, opp. p. 59, but a distant view of the west face of the screen is given in Turner's Interior of Ely Cathedral in Aberdeen Art Gallery (Turner exhibition catalogue, Tate Gallery London, 1974, pl. 13). A section is in W. Stevenson, op. cit., opp. p. 74.
28. This involved the loss of a curious pinnacle or flèche which seems Jacobean (Pl. XVIIB); it could date from Laudian repairs under Bishop Matthew Wren in the 1630s or it could, more likely, date from the post-Interregnum repairs; cf. the new canopy on the Swynford tombs at Lincoln which dates from this period.
29. They did however ensure the careful reburial in Bishop West's chapel of the remains of the seven Saxon notables incorporated in the north wall of the Norman choir. Bentham, 285–86.
30. Ely Diocesan Archives D/9/9.

Sutton in the Isle of Ely and its Architectural Context

By RICHARD FAWCETT

INTRODUCTION

The church of St Andrew at Sutton, one of the most splendid of the 14th-century churches in the Isle of Ely, is generally considered to be characteristic of its area for the use it makes of architectural features which had been — or were to be — employed in other buildings of northern Cambridgeshire. However, a search for parallels has suggested that the most immediate and precise contemporary relationships of the first phase of the building are with a small group of parish churches in central Norfolk, and since these relationships provide an instructive demonstration of the spread of architectural ideas through the eastern counties, they may be thought worthy of examination.

DESCRIPTION OF SUTTON

Sutton is a large church with a three-bay aisle-less choir, a six-bay aisled nave, a two-storey south porch, and a western tower.[1] It is usually stated that it was erected in one extended building campaign, but close examination suggests that there were three separate, principal phases of construction. A continuous base course runs around choir, nave and porch, and shows that they were planned and set out in a single operation, but there is a clear difference of character between the choir and nave above the base course, from which it is evident that one was completed by a second architect. On the basis of analogy with related buildings it will be argued here that the nave details, including the base course, are homogeneous in character, and therefore represent the first building phase. From this it follows that it was the choir which was completed in a second campaign by a later architect.[2] The tower, which was the last major addition to the church, rises above a base course of a different profile from that around the rest of the church and its details point to a third building campaign datable to the 15th century.

The only reasonably securely dated parts of the church are the nave and its contemporary south porch. For these a range of dates is indicated by the heraldry of the porch vaulting bosses, which may be interpreted as those of the two bishops who occupied the See of Ely during the course of construction.[3] The earlier of the arms are those of John Barnet, bishop from 1366 to 1373, followed by those of his successor, Thomas FitzAlan, or Arundel,[4] who was bishop of Ely until his elevation to York in 1388. Since the arms of York are also shown, the porch vault, which would have been one of the last parts of this first building campaign, must date from after 1388, although the church as a whole appears to have been started between 1366 and 1373. How far this heraldry can be taken as an indication of personal interest in the building by these bishops is uncertain. The rectory was appropriated to the Hosteller of Ely cathedral priory, and a vicarage was ordained in 1254,[5] which presumably resulted in the priory having responsibility for the fabric of the choir. On this basis alone there is no reason to assume any involvement by the bishops in the construction of the nave, although the inclusion of the arms of York might be thought too precise a reference to Bishop Arundel to be dismissed.

Externally, the most prominent feature of the church is the telescoped two-stage octagonal superstructure of the tower, which provides a landmark over several miles of the Fenland country. On closer inspection an equally noteworthy feature is the south flank of the nave, which is entirely faced with ashlar, and is elaborated by a series of extraordinary polygonal swellings at the junction of the buttresses and wall for which no precise parallel is known. Such profligate display of ashlar, in an area which had to import all its freestone, was denied to the north nave flank, which presumably has always been less in the public gaze; like the choir it is of rubble. As usual in the greater 14th-century churches of this area the principal decorative focus is the window tracery. In the three-light windows of the nave aisles the tracery is a variant on the configuration of four diagonally-disposed daggers (Fig. 3c). The choir has more unusual forms. In the north and south walls the three-light windows have super-arches containing daggers over the side lights, with a pair of cusped leaf forms to either side of a supermullion, and a flattened dagger in the central field. The five-light east window is sub-arcuated into a 2–1–2 grouping, with basically reticulated forms within the sub-arches, and a hybrid combination of curvilinear and rectilinear forms in the central field. A transom crosses the mullions at rather less than half their height. There is a marked contrast between the types of tracery employed in the nave and choir; whereas the architect of the nave appears to have been chiefly interested in the contained forms of the tracery, the architect of the choir was concerned to create essentially linear patterns, within which the contained forms are almost incidental. The tentative rectilinearity of the choir tracery may be taken as supporting evidence that its design was later than that of the nave.

Internally, the tall arcades of the nave are carried on piers which are extended along their north–south axis to an elongated lozenge type of plan which was to be favoured in a number of the larger later medieval churches of the eastern counties (Fig. 7a).[6] Corresponding to the arcades are blind arches along the inner walls of the aisles, by means of which the rhythm established in the arcade is reflected throughout the church. The aisle walls are further articulated by a string-course running beneath the windows. One other internal feature worthy of remark is the piscina in the south-east angle of the south aisle: this feature is set diagonally across the angle within an arch capped by a pair of ogees, above which rises a tabernacle containing a seated figure.

Several elements in the design of the church can be taken as indicative of local influence or preference: most obviously, the western tower is plainly at home in a region which showed a long-lived partiality for octagonal structures.[7] Internally, both the elongated form of the piers and the use of wall arcades invite comparison with other churches in the immediate area in which these features are to be found,[8] although the difficulty of tracing precise relationships of detail renders the majority of these local comparisons of general rather than specific value. Of more particular interest are those elements which might indicate a debt to the work at the cathedral priory. These include the piscina and tabernacle in the south aisle, in which may be detected an awareness of related features in the Lady chapel and in Prior Crauden's chapel, and the nave tracery, which may show a debt to the tracery screens within the gallery openings of the cathedral choir. It requires no more than a sporadic knowledge of the churches of the eastern counties to appreciate that the 14th-century work at the cathedral was looked to for inspiration over several decades, and so it is easy to accept that Ely was indeed an important influence on nearby Sutton. However, closer acquaintance with the churches throughout the region suggests that there is a very complex pattern of cross-fertilisation of ideas along what might be termed the 'Ely–Norwich axis', and it is essential to take this into account before too readily assuming one particular source for an element.

DESCRIPTION OF RELATED CHURCHES

The churches with which the first phase of Sutton shows the closest relationships are all within central Norfolk: they are the nave and north transept chapel of Attleborough, the nave of Little Cressingham, the choir of Hingham and the choir of Wilby. If Sutton's apparent links with this group can be sustained through precise comparisons of detail, one concrete instance of the dissemination of architectural ideas along this axis will have been identified. Before considering the details of these buildings in relation to Sutton each will be described briefly.

St Mary, Attleborough is a large and complex building, despite the destruction of its choir in about 1541.[9] The earliest parts of the surviving fabric are the Romanesque central tower piers, to the south of which is the transept chapel of St Mary, founded under a bequest by Sir William Mortimer of 1297.[10] The parts of the church which are of immediate concern, however, are the aisled nave, the north transept chapel, and the earliest parts of the north porch, for all of which there is a rather confusing variety of documentary evidence. The nave is usually dated to 1387, although it has sometimes been placed after 1405.[11] In support of the earlier date is Sir Robert Mortimer's foundation of a college of the Holy Cross in the Church, for which he bequeathed 2,000 marks with the direction that the college was to consist of a master and four chaplains. However, the requisite royal license for this was not granted until 1405,[12] and this has led some writers to place this later date on the building. Yet it seems certain that the construction of the nave was not directly linked with the establishment of the college, for which accommodation was provided at the east end of the church,[13] and there are structural indications that the nave was started considerably before 1387. The evidence is to be seen in the relationship of the north transept chapel, which was built before 1379,[14] with the nave. Since the former is not coursed-in with the aisle wall, but is simply abutted against it, the chapel can be seen to post-date the aisle, and the

FIG. 1. Distribution map showing Sutton and related churches

latter is therefore anterior to 1379.[15] Nevertheless, chapel and nave are certainly the work of the same architect since the details are identical, and so the construction of the two parts is unlikely to be separated by any great gap of time. In any consideration of Attleborough two later building operations must also be taken into account. The north porch, although probably set out at the same time as the nave in view of the similarity of their base courses, was eventually constructed by Sir John Ratcliffe, who died in 1441.[16] Of greater significance for the present appearance of the church was the work of John Ratcliffe, Lord Fitz-Walter, who raised the outer walls of the aisles and chapels, and rebuilt the roofs to a flatter pitch at some date before 1495,[17] thus causing a detrimental change to the internal proportions.

St Andrew, Hingham, like Sutton and Attleborough, is a large church. As at Sutton the plan is composed of an aisle-less choir, an aisled nave, a south porch and a western tower. Unfortunately there is no firm evidence for its date, although there is a strong and constantly repeated tradition that it was entirely rebuilt whilst Remigius of Hethersett was rector, that is, between 1316 and 1359.[18] Nave and choir must certainly be ascribed to different architects, the former probably being a decade or more earlier than the latter. Remigius's personal interest in the fabric as rector was presumably confined to the choir, if he was indeed the instigator of its construction, but this tradition can give nothing more exact than a *terminus ante quem* of 1359 for the commencement of work on this part of the building.

The churches of *St Andrew, Little Cressingham* and *All Saints, Wilby* are smaller buildings than the others under consideration, and there appears to be no documentary evidence for the dates of their construction. The aisle-less choir of Little Cressingham is the earliest part of that building, to which the four-bay aisled nave, with a tower-porch in its south-west bay, was added in a second campaign. The nave and tower have been in a semi-ruinous state since the late 16th century,[19] and the present good repair of the two eastern bays of the nave is a result of the granting of a faculty for repairing half the structure in 1781.[20] Wilby church is made up of an aisle-less choir and nave, with a south porch and west tower. Despite its small size the choir is finely proportioned, showing a notable sensitivity on the part of its architect.

RELATIONSHIPS OF TRACERY

Since the window tracery of Sutton nave is one of its most conspicuous features it may be taken as a starting point in considering the relationships between Sutton and the other churches. Tracery composed of four diagonally set daggers had first appeared in the eastern counties virtually simultaneously at the cathedrals of Norwich and Ely in the early 1320s (Fig. 2a and c). At Norwich it is found in the south walk of the cloister, probably started in about 1322,[21] where it was employed with a variant in which four daggers are set in a cruciform manner (Fig. 2b). The two types alternate along the length of the walk. At Ely, where the choir was rebuilt by Bishop Hotham after the collapse of the tower in February 1322,[22] the diagonal pattern is found in five of the six arches of the gallery; significantly, the south-west bay of the gallery, which was almost certainly the first to be built,[23] has tracery with the cruciform pattern of daggers — as at Norwich the two types appear to have been designed as complementary variants (Fig. 2d).

There can be little doubt that the tracery types used at Norwich and Ely are related, and there are good reasons to believe that each designer was aware of what his counterpart was doing; yet there is an emphatic difference in their detailed treatment which plainly marks the two works as being by different architects. At Norwich the overall treatment is robust and simple; it is characteristic of the design that ogee curves are employed only for the main light arches, or where they are virtually unavoidable. By contrast, at Ely the containing framework is wilfully curved around the subordinated tracery in an extraordinarily sinuous manner, and there is a filigree delicacy which is entirely alien to the Norwich work. This delicacy is seen most obviously in the gallery tracery of the south-west bay, where the dagger forms are intricately curved so that their formpieces are contiguous and interlocking as far as possible, and further complexity is introduced by the insertion of miniscule loops into the interstices between the forms. It might be argued that such unusually rich tracery as that at Ely could only have been produced as a unique response to the opportunities presented to the architect at this prestigious operation, and that he would have tended to revert to

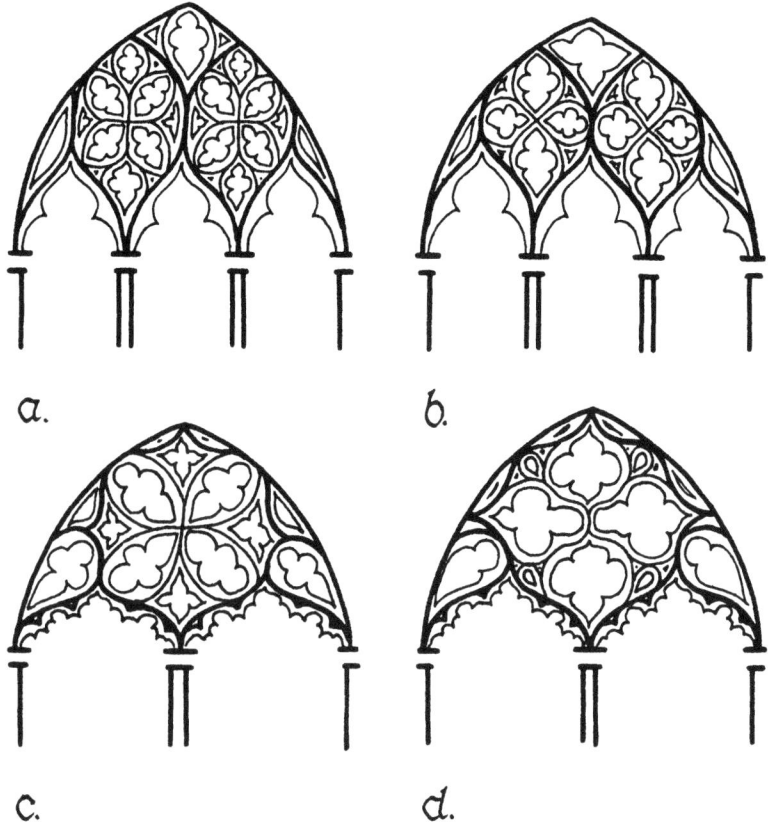

Fig. 2. Tracery designs
(a) and (b) Norwich cathedral: cloister, S range
(c) and (d) Ely cathedral: choir gallery

more sober — and less expensive — designs at a less lavishly financed operation. However, such an argument is rendered untenable by the fact that very similar tracery, some of which is yet more opulently rich in detail, is to be found in a small number of parish churches in the eastern counties, some of which must certainly be attributed to the same architect.[24] In view of this it is important to see the Ely tracery as indicative of a personal style, and not simply as a one-off speciality.

Although the 14th-century work at both Ely and Norwich can be shown to have had some immediate following in parochial architecture, it is generally true to say that the influence of these two buildings tended to be disseminated relatively slowly. Tracery of the basic configuration under consideration was to have a limited vogue over a wide area (Fig. 3), although the chief concentration is certainly in the eastern counties, particularly in Norfolk,[25] but there appear to be no firmly datable parochial examples before the central decades of the century. By the time it was used at Sutton, Attleborough and Hingham the idea was

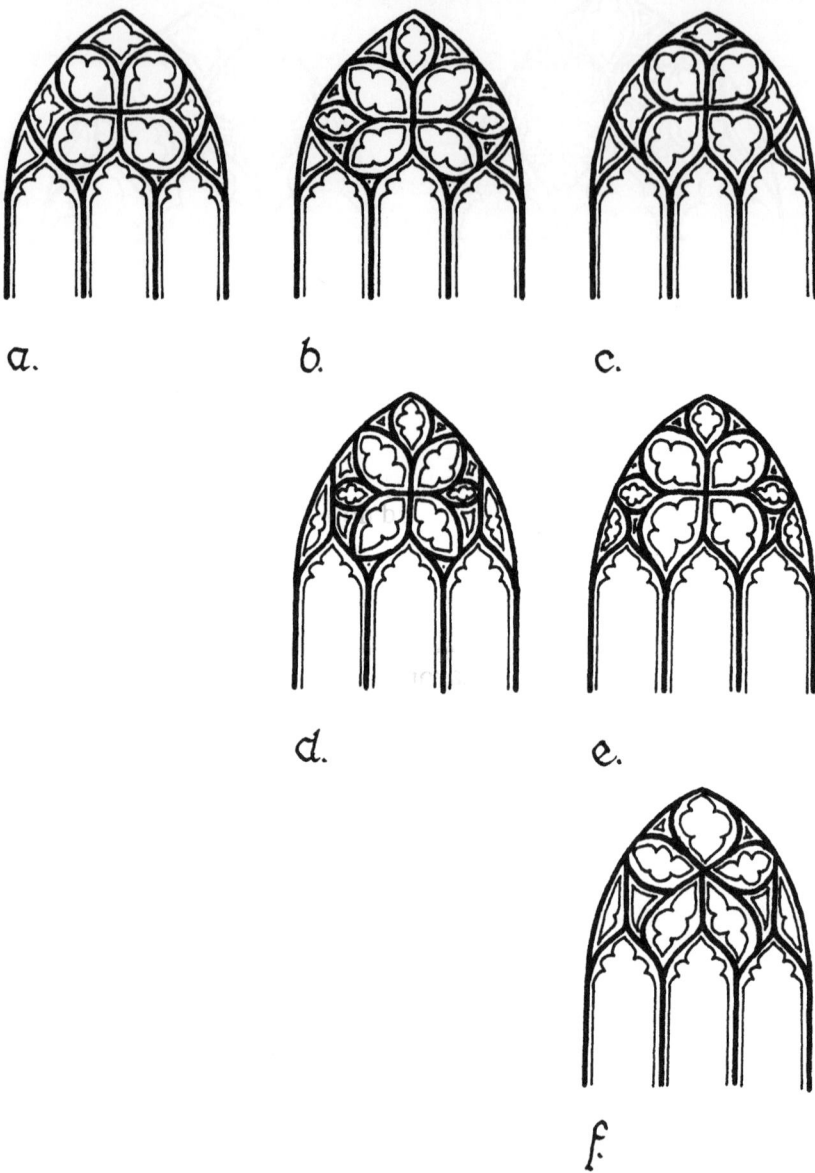

Fig. 3. Parochial variants of tracery designs with diagonal combinations of dagger forms

(a) Attleborough, Beetley, Hevingham, St Michael Coslany, Norwich
(b) Hingham
(c) Sutton
(d) Acle, Aylmerton, Hickling, Taverham, Weasenham St Peter
(e) Wangford (Suffolk), Postwick (with differences)
(f) Laxfield (Suffolk), Hevingham (Suffolk) (with differences)

already thirty or more years old, yet there are surprisingly few examples of the type which could be dated with much confidence between the 1320s and 1350s.[26] It is therefore hard to escape the conclusion that the mid-century works were looking back to one of the cathedrals rather than to an intermediary building. The fundamental simplicity of the majority of the parochial examples, and their concentration in Norfolk, makes it appear likely that it was Norwich to which they were looking rather than Ely. In this group of buildings the tracery of Hingham choir is closest to the prototype of Norwich in having additional daggers which develop between the main ones (Fig. 3b), and although the Hingham type has no precise counterparts elsewhere, a modified version is found in at least five other churches in Norfolk, one of which, Acle (Fig. 3d), has a date which might be seen as supporting the traditional pre-1359 date of Hingham.[27] The simplest version of this tracery is found at Attleborough (Fig. 3a), where no additional forms are included between the daggers, and the interstices are merely cusped; other windows in Norfolk, at Beetley, Hevingham and Norwich are very similar. The tracery of Sutton (Fig. 3c) is closer in spirit to Attleborough than Hingham, except that its lower daggers are deflected downwards between the light heads, and in this it displays some kinship with more complex examples in Suffolk at Wangford, Laxfield and Hevingham, and in Norfolk at Postwick (Fig. 3e and f).

The same diagonal configuration was also employed within the five-light west window of Attleborough (Fig. 4a). This window is sub-arcuated into two intersecting groups of three lights, with diagonal daggers radiating from the super-arch apex at the centre of the two divisions, and with a cruciform configuration of daggers at the head of the tracery.[28] It is to be regretted that the tracery of Hingham east window has not survived since it was planned on an equally generous scale as the west window at Attleborough, and may possibly have shown similar forms.[29] The three-light east window of Wilby (Fig. 4b), although much smaller, is nevertheless a fine composition which shows links with Attleborough in the use of an intersecting matrix for the subordinated tracery, and in the cruciform combinations of daggers. A further significant comparison may be seen in the use of an interlocking combination, composed of a dagger and a pair of twisted mouchettes, above the ogee light-heads at both Wilby and Attleborough; similar combinations were also used in the two-light aisle end windows of Attleborough (Fig. 4c), and in the central light of the nave windows of Little Cressingham (Fig. 4d). This last window type is one of the most curious to be found in all this group of churches. The window arch is of four-centred form — an unusually early instance of this arch for Norfolk — and each of the lights rises up to the soffit of the main arch, from which the side light arches take their centres. The only tracery in the window is introduced at a subordinate level beneath the head of the central light. At Attleborough a strikingly similar type of window is used in the nave clerestory (Fig. 4e), except that the central light tracery is reduced to a dagger above a depressed two-centred arch.

It cannot be claimed that the evidence of the tracery alone indicates any more than a strong possibility of kinship between Sutton, Attleborough, Hingham, Little Cressingham and Wilby; all that can be safely concluded on these grounds is that there is nothing which could be considered inconsistent with kinship. In considering the details of the mouldings, however, it is possible to be more precise. If there is a clear resemblance between the same features at two or more buildings, particularly if these features show profiles which suggest a markedly individualistic approach to their design, the cumulative evidence for relationship is more acceptable. Having discussed the window tracery the details of the window reveals may be taken as a starting point in considering the mouldings.

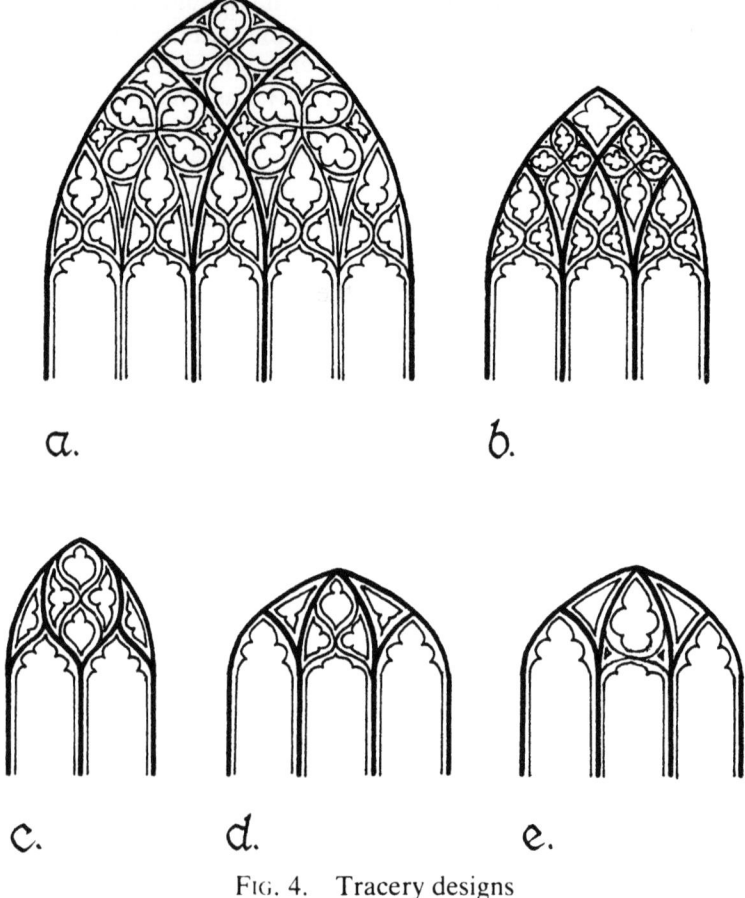

FIG. 4. Tracery designs
(a) Attleborough, W window
(b) Wilby, E Window
(c) Attleborough, aisles, W end
(d) Little Cressingham, aisle flanks
(e) Attleborough, clerestory

RELATIONSHIPS OF MOULDINGS

At all five churches under consideration the tracery is recessed within the thickness of the wall on a plane which is expressed as a narrow border running around the window at the same depth as the leading faces of the mullions, but which is carefully distinguished from the half-mullions absorbed into the reveals by a quirk (Fig. 5). From this plane the reveals project at ninety degrees towards the wall face before being cut back in a broad chamfer into which a continuous moulding is cut. The only exception to this is at Wilby (Fig. 5e), where the east window mouldings are further elaborated by a half-round hollow cut into the face of the reveal which runs at ninety degrees to the window plane. The continuous moulding cut into the chamfered plane of the reveals is a simple casement at four of these churches, but at Little Cressingham a wave moulding is employed instead at this point (Fig. 5d). It will be found that these two mouldings figure elsewhere in these churches, and, although common mouldings in themselves, the particular uses made of them in these instances may be seen as significant. The profile of the mullions, although in no sense unique, is also sufficiently striking to call for comment. By the second half of the 14th century mullions were generally cut with hollowed flanks, possibly because this had the visual effect of reducing the apparent substance of the masonry. In these churches, however, there is a firm preference for a clear expression of planes, which is evident in the straight angled flanks of the mullions, interrupted only by the asymmetrical quirk which separates

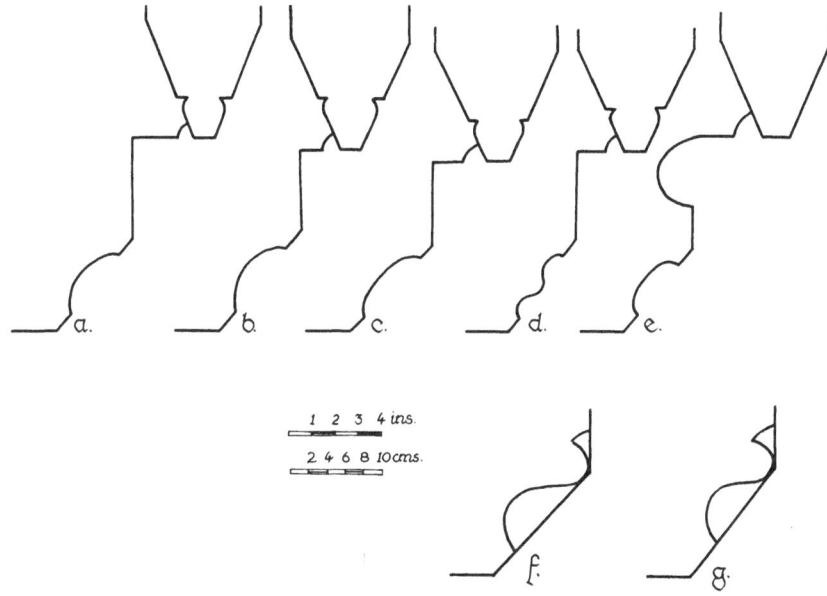

FIG. 5. Profiles of window mouldings
(a) Attleborough, nave, reveals
(b) Hingham, choir, reveals
(c) Sutton, nave, reveals
(d) Little Cressingham, nave, reveals
(e) Wilby, E window reveals
(f) Hingham, choir, rere-arches
(g) Attleborough, W window rere-arch

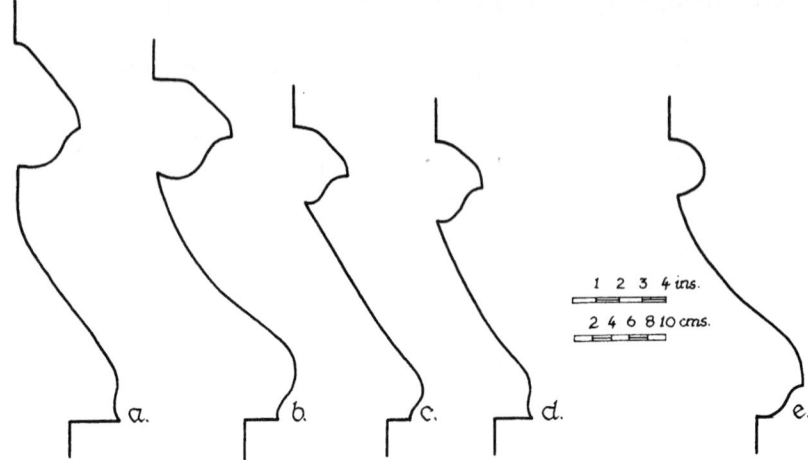

FIG. 6. External base courses
(a) Attleborough, nave and transepts
(b) Wilby, choir
(c) Sutton, nave, porch and choir
(d) Little Cressingham, nave
(e) Hingham, choir

the leading moulding from the main body of the mullion, at all but Wilby. An additional link between the windows in two of these churches may be found at Hingham and Attleborough: the north and south windows of the former, and the west window of the latter having a simple moulding to the rear-arches which is clearly comparable (Fig. 5f and g).

As a general rule, examination of the mouldings of external base courses tends to be unrewarding in any search for relationships between buildings. Their design called for little inventiveness, and, since they have usually suffered most immediately from several centuries of weathering, they are often so badly decayed or so over-restored that the profile is of little value. Where positive kinship can be found in the form of this feature at a group of churches, therefore, it is a welcome bonus, and seldom more so than in this group, where the mouldings, with one exception, are unusual and yet have much in common with each other (Fig. 6). As well as the obvious visual function of making a building appear well-founded, a base course was intended to project the water which ran down the wall face away from the foot of the wall, and to this end it was usually provided with a projecting neb at the foot of the sequence of mouldings. At Sutton, Attleborough, Wilby and Little Cressingham this neb is reduced to a salient arris, whilst the under surface of the lower moulding is completely flat, with no hollow to prevent water running back to the wall face. The form this moulding takes, along with the general angularity of the whole formation at each church, is strong presumptive evidence for inter-relationship; the only exception to this is Hingham (Fig. 6e), where there may have been extensive re-cutting in the course of restoration.

DESIGN OF ARCADES

However, it is in the similarity of design to be seen in the nave arcades of the three aisled churches, Sutton, Little Cressingham and Attleborough, that the greatest interest of this group must be seen to lie. Accepting dates of before 1373 for Sutton, and before 1379 for Attleborough, these buildings are almost certainly the earliest datable examples in East Anglia to possess the type of pier which was extended along its north–south axis rather than symmetrical about both axes. If these two, and Little Cressingham, can be shown to be related, together they provide important evidence for the early development of such piers, which were to be employed by several of the more imaginative architects of the eastern counties up to the close of the Middle Ages.

It is generally claimed that the motive behind the development of piers of this type was the desire to pare down the supporting elements to the minimum size which could effectively discharge its function, and so to reduce the spatial separation of aisles and central vessel. But, in the early examples at least, the physical mass of such piers is frequently considerably greater than that of a conventionally designed pier. By extending the piers along their north–south axis to the full width of the wall or beyond, such piers are wider than they might otherwise have been, since parochial piers were generally narrower than the wall they support. In fact it seems that a number of architects working on parish churches in the region were becoming increasingly preoccupied with the nature of the relationship between pier, arch and supported wall from about the second quarter of the 14th century onwards, and it was this which led to the emergence of a new pier type. It appears that these architects were concerned to develop a means of integrating their piers into the internal elevations, so that they continued to be identifiable as a distinct and separately defined supporting element, and at the same time could be seen as a part of the wall itself. In Norfolk the earliest attempt to achieve something of this on a parochial scale was probably at Snettisham, in the north-east corner of the county.[30] At this church the basically quatrefoil form of the piers was augmented with triple-filleted rolls between the lobes, which were made to pass unbroken through the capitals to continue around the arches and down into the adjacent piers. But the piers and arches at Snettisham are an almost exact repetition on a smaller scale of the Ely cathedral choir arcades, and this close similarity, which extends to the tracery, makes it very likely that the same architect was responsible for the design of both buildings. Because of its immediate debt to ideas developed at Ely, Snettisham is exceptional, although related experiments may be seen slightly later at a number of other churches in Norfolk, and particularly in a group in the centre of the county, including Great Walsingham and Beeston St Mary, all of which appear to be the work of one architect.[31] In this group the intermediate mouldings of the quatrefoil piers were extended into the capitals and down into the bases to give a unity to the pier as a whole, but the only continuity into the arches was created by a series of vertical faces which reflected the form of the abacus before dying into the arch mouldings. The arches, therefore, remained essentially separate.

However, the designs adopted at Sutton, Attleborough and Little Cressingham (Fig. 7) were very different from these earlier experiments. As has been said, the core of these piers is extended to the full width of the supported wall, with a broad strip on the north and south sides which may be understood as an expression of the wall face. The only shafts are those on the east and west sides of the piers where they have the function of supporting the inner order of the arches. The pier flanks are partly cut away at an angle at Sutton and Little Cressingham, and these angled faces are relieved by the same mouldings as were noted in the external window reveals: a wave at Cressingham and a casement at Sutton. At Attleborough (Fig. 7c) the transition between the east and west shafts and the north and south faces is made by an ogee curve rather than by canted faces, so that the constituent elements are less clearly defined. But the basic similarity of the solution adopted in the piers at all these churches is abundantly clear in the arches, in which all of the mouldings of the pier flanks, apart from the engaged shafts which are stopped by capitals, are carried through unbroken into the arch.

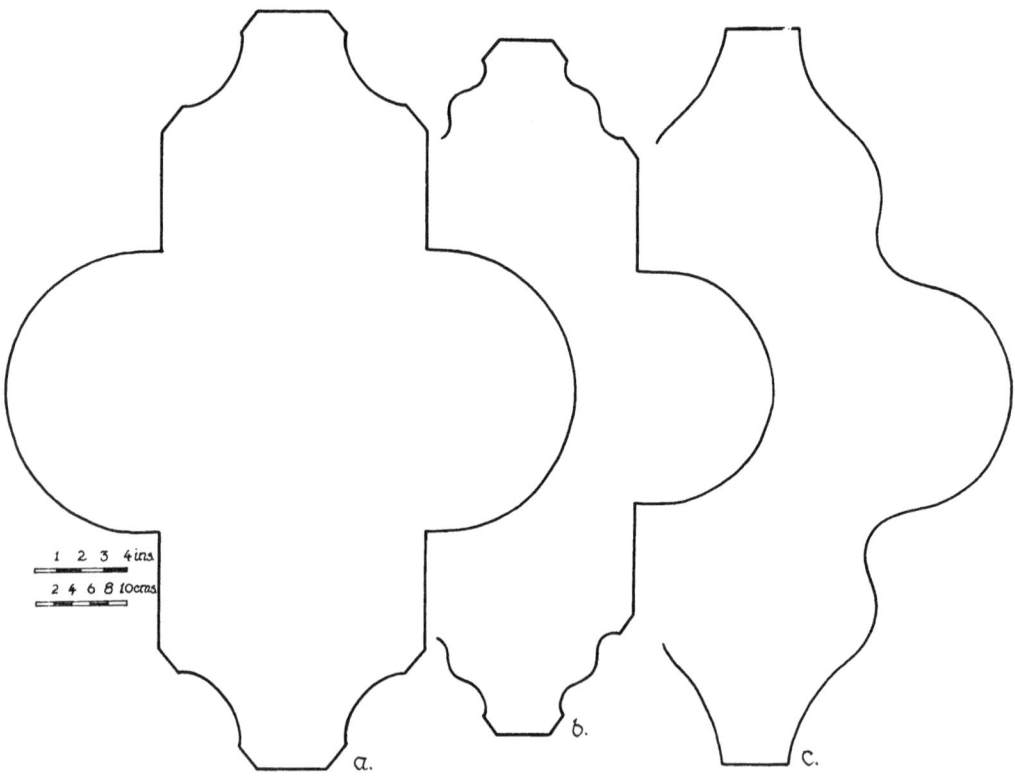

FIG. 7. Sections of arcade piers
    (a) Sutton
    (b) Little Cressingham
    (c) Attleborough

One other architect was working in a similar vein in Norfolk at about the same time, and he designed the nave of Swanton Morley, a church which was probably started slightly later than the buildings under discussion.[32] At Swanton Morley the piers also have flat faces to north and south which are continued up into the supported wall, and engaged shafts to east and west; they also have the appearance of being longer along their north–south axis, although this is in fact an illusion, and the piers may be understood as having a very cleverly modified quatrefoil section. In view of the subtlety of this solution it seems certain that the architect's chief concern was not simply to reduce the dimensions of the pier — for this he could have adopted much simpler expedients — but to express the pier as a constituent element of the wall, with the only relic of the pier as a separated element surviving in the shafts which support the inner arcade order. Significantly none of these early examples has shafts to north and south, as was to become usual later, and as a result the plane of the wall is particularly clearly expressed in the pier. At Swanton Morley this is even more evident in the south arcade than the north, since the former has no projecting hood mould above the arches to interrupt the continuity between the piers and the clerestory wall. Perhaps it might not be too grandiloquent to claim for the development seen in these churches that they are a much later parochial parallel for what Panofsky found in the nave of S. Denis, where the architect 'chose to sacrifice the columnar principle' in order to establish 'adequate representation of the nave wall by the core of the pier'.[33]

To reinforce the idea that the pier was indeed an integral part of the wall, and at the same time part of a logical and complete system of wall and support, at Sutton, Attleborough and Little Cressingham there are wall arcades along the aisle walls corresponding to the main arcades.[34] There can be no serious contention that a wall arcade has any practical advantage in an unvaulted parish church: the saving of materials in the thinner sections of wall enclosed by the arches was more than offset by the cost of the freestone necessary for responds and arches, particularly in a region which had no native freestone. Where such arches are employed it is evident that the architect's chief concern was to relate the rhythm established by the main arcades to an overall system of spatial sub-division which encompassed the whole interior of the building. The responds of the wall arcades in these churches were designed as reduced versions of that part of the pier which was continued into the outer order of the arches, and which was thus most immediately related to the supported wall. At the same time the scale of the arches was linked to the proportions of the aisles, and consequently they spring from a lower point than the main arcade arches. This also allowed sufficient pitch for the slope of the aisle roofs. Regrettably, at Attleborough the effect of the wall arcades has been marred by the heightening of the aisle walls and the construction of flatter roofs than those originally built. This has resulted in large expanses of blank walling above the apices of the wall arcade, which are unrelated to the dominant rhythm of arches.

In the design of the other details of the piers we again find close similarity although not identity between the group of churches under discussion. This is

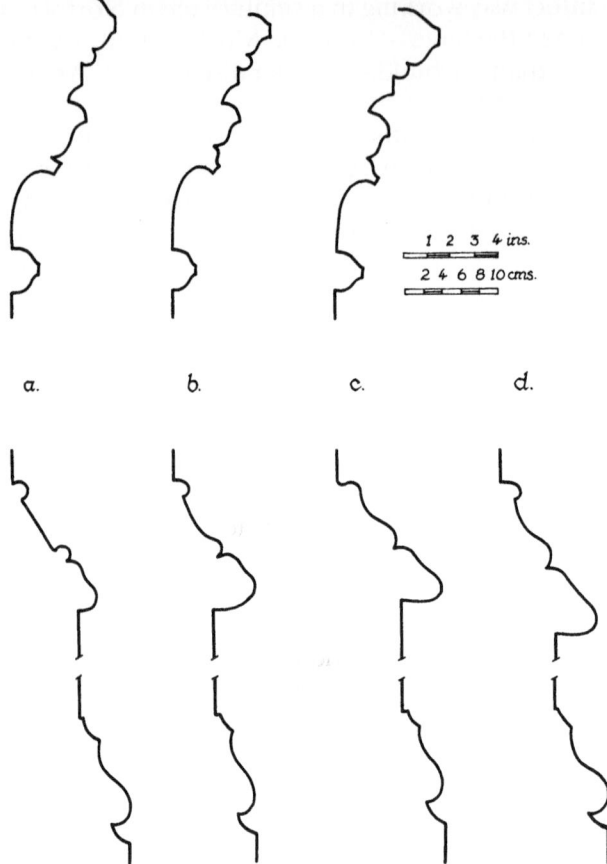

FIG. 8. Profiles of capitals and bases
(a) Attleborough
(b) Little Cressingham
(c) Sutton (based on section provided by Dr R. K. Morris)
(d) Ely cathedral, N choir arcade

particularly true of the capitals (Fig. 8), which are variants of the most common 14th-century East Anglian form. However, the bases are worthy of rather more detailed comment. At all three churches there is a simple polygonal sub-base in two stages, the upper one of which is articulated in four parts corresponding to the major elements in the pier, and is finished off by an ogee moulding terminating in a hollow chamfer. The main body of the pier develops above this point, although the engaged shafts have additional individual bases, consisting of a semi-octagonal stock and a widely projecting semi-circular moulding in two parts of bell-like profile.[35] Again we are reminded that the shafts are the only residue of the 'columnar principle'.

The ingenuity involved in designing the complex relationship between the parts of these bases has no satisfactory local precedent, and must be seen as the architect's own response to the particular problems of the pier he had designed. However, it is just possible that the later base form which is found in the two piers of the north arcade of Ely cathedral choir may have had some influence on the design of the Sutton bases (Fig. 8d).[36] These bases, like those of Sutton (Fig. 8c), have widely projecting bell-like upper mouldings of pronouncedly Late Gothic form, and they are also given a more complex appearance than the others in the choir arcades since the intermediate pier mouldings are allowed to penetrate downwards, rather than being stopped by subordinate bases. Frankl has suggested that Late Gothic bases 'give the impression that the piers do not stand on any clearly delineated supports, but that the shafts have grown side by side at their own tempo',[37] and there is already something of this quality in the Ely choir north piers, which may have helped the architect of Sutton to work out his own solutions.

CONCLUSION

The evidence of the tracery, mouldings and arcades of this group of parish churches would seem to be sufficient to place their inter-relationship beyond doubt, and such a conclusion is reinforced by what must be seen as a very similar attitude to overall design, particularly in the use of wall arcades. On this evidence it may be suggested that the same creative mind was responsible for the design of each, assuming that the idea of individual creativity in medieval architecture is valid. The manner in which the problems of design are solved in each church is so alike in detail — and at the same time so unlike the solutions devised at most contemporary churches in the region — that it is difficult to conceive of any more satisfactory hypothesis than common authorship.

A prime source of inspiration for the architect was certainly the work at the two cathedral priories of Norwich and Ely. The window tracery relies on forms employed in the Norwich cloister, whilst the more fanciful elements, such as the piscina and surmounting niche at Sutton, show an awareness of the tabernacle work in Ely Lady chapel. It has also been suggested that the pier bases may show some debt to Ely choir, although here the personal ingenuity of the architect must certainly be given full credit. From this it is apparent that well into the third quarter of the 14th century the great cathedral and abbey lodges continued to provide fresh stimuli drawn from the larger architectural world. This must be seen as one reason for an inherent conservatism which may be detected in certain aspects of the design of these churches. It should be remembered that Ely choir had been completed by 1338, and the Lady chapel eleven years later,[38] whilst the tracery of the south walk of Norwich cloister was probably designed as early as 1322.[39] Furthermore there was relatively little major building between those years and the reconstruction of Norwich cathedral choir clerestory in the 1360s.[40] The personal style of the architect of this group had probably reached maturity in the 1350s under the influence of the most recently completed great buildings in the region — although these were by then twenty or thirty years old — and it is true to say that it shows no real development in the buildings under discussion. His inventiveness and ingenuity are unquestionable within the limits of his personal style, but they are confined to problems which he had already identified, and he appears to have been reticent in confronting new problems.

His reticence is most obvious in his failure to be influenced by the rectilinear tracery which at last reached Norfolk — albeit in a somewhat garbled form — in the clerestory of Norwich cathedral, at a time when some of these churches may not yet have been started. The architects of Swanton Morley nave and Aylsham north transept,[41] for example, took up these new tracery forms shortly afterwards, but presumably they were younger men who were more receptive to fresh stimuli and whose ideas were not yet fixed. The work of the architect of Sutton suggests a designer who was highly resourceful with the vocabulary of forms which he had derived from the best exemplars available to him. These he used with great thoughtfulness, but he was nevertheless largely unaware of architectural thought outside his sphere of activity, and consequently tended to be unable to come to terms with new ideas once his style had been formed. If this is a true picture of one parochial architect, whose detectable influence suggests he was something of a leader in the eastern counties, it is understandable that when, from the later 14th century, the great foundations were increasingly unable to provide the architectural authority which they had once had, parochial architecture should have tended to become more introverted and regional in character.

REFERENCES

1. The modern sacristy is excluded from this discussion, although it appears that a medieval building existed on its site.
2. The two most valuable published descriptions of Sutton, VCH, *Cambridge and the Isle of Ely*, IV (London 1953), and B/E, *Cambridgeshire*, 2nd ed. (1970), both suggest that the choir pre-dates the nave within one extended building campaign.
3. VCH, op. cit., 161 seq.
4. A son of the Earl of Arundel.
5. J. Bentham, 147 seq. Amongst the other rectories appropriated to the Hosteller were those of Witchford and Meldreth, Seiriol Evans, *The Mediaeval Estate of the Cathedral Priory of Ely* (Ely 1973), 9.
6. See B/E, *Cambridgeshire*, 274–75.
7. On his distribution maps T. D. Atkinson, *Local Style in English Architecture* (London 1947), shows a heavy concentration of polygonal towers in Cambridgeshire. Although the octagon at Ely cathedral plainly inspired a number of 14th- and 15th-century examples in the area, the tradition had been established earlier, as is shown by the Romanesque octagonal superstructure of Swaffham Prior tower.
8. VCH, op. cit., 162.
9. It was demolished by Henry, Earl of Sussex, and its materials 'conuerted and ymployed to the sayd Earles use upon his house' according to the returns for Bishop Redman's visitation of 1602 (*The East Anglian*, I (1864), 340 and 370, and II (1866), 75, 89, 223 and 231).
10. Francis Blomefield, *Essay Towards a Topographical History of the County of Norfolk*, 2nd ed. (1805–10), I, 509 and 527.
11. T. Hugh Bryant, *The Churches of Norfolk, Hundred of Shropham* (Norwich 1913), 35.
12. R.L.P. 7, Henry IV, pt. ii m. 22.
13. The Earl of Sussex demolished the choir on the pretext that it was associated with the college, although the 1602 returns (see above note 9) specifically stated that the 'Chancell . . . was

adioyned to a Chappell belonginge to a Colledge of Preeists or Chantry there'. Nevertheless, the founder also had an interest in the structure of the nave since his arms are recorded in its glazing (Blomefield, op. cit.).
14. The north transept was built in the lifetime of Thomas Chanticler (d. 1379) who directed in his will that he was to be buried in it (Norwich Consistory Court Wills, 162 Heydon).
15. I owe the information on the lack of bond to Mr Arthur Whittingham, who informs me that this was even more evident before the church was repaired some years ago.
16. The arms of Ratcliffe quartering Mortimer are over the door: Sir John's father had married Cecily, second daughter of Sir Thomas Mortimer.
17. He placed his own arms and those of his wife, daughter of Sir Richard Whetehill of Calais, on the roof; he was subsequently attainted and beheaded in 1495. See Arthur Whittingham, *Archaeol. J.*, CVI (1949).
18. Blomefield, op. cit., II, 424.
19. According to the 1602 visitation (see above note 9) the roof on the north 'lyeth wyde open', and the tower was 'much decayed and ruinated'.
20. J. Charles Cox, *County Churches, Norfolk* (London 1911), I, 61.
21. E. C. Fernie and A. B. Whittingham, *The Early Communar . . . Rolls of Norwich Cathedral Priory* (Norfolk Record Society, XLI), 1972, 34.
22. Stewart, 82.
23. There is a marked change of design beyond this bay, and its pier is unlike the others of the choir in having a sequence of mouldings like that of the octagon piers.
24. These include Grantchester choir (Cambs.), Snettisham, Heacham W window, Terrington St John nave clerestory, and the top stage of the S tower of Kings Lynn St Margaret (Norf.). See brief discussion of this type of tracery in Richard Fawcett, *Later Gothic Architecture in Norfolk*, unpublished Ph.D. thesis (University of East Anglia 1975), 139–49.
25. A particularly puzzling exception to this is its occurrence in two-light windows in the tower of Edington church, Wilts., built by Bishop Edington of Winchester between 1352 and 1361.
26. The Great Gate of Bury St Edmunds abbey has related tracery in its east face at first-floor level, which may be one of the earliest surviving examples. However, although this gate was started c. 1327, it was still unfinished by 1353, and in view of its position this window may belong to a late stage in the building operation.
27. Acle choir is known to have been built by a rector who died in 1362. See C. L. S. Linnell, 'The Commonplace Book of Robert Reynys of Acle', *Norfolk Archaeology*, XXXII (1958–61), 124.
28. It should be mentioned that the east window of Soham, Cambs., shows similarities to the Attleborough west window, and the nave windows are related to those of Attleborough clerestory; and there is consequently a possible link between the churches. However, I have had no opportunity to examine the 14th-century remodelling of Soham in detail.
29. It was destroyed to make way for the present startlingly inappropriate tracery after the patron of the parish, Lord Wodehouse, presented the church with a fine collection of German glass in 1813.
30. See Richard Fawcett, op. cit., 121 seq.
31. See Richard Fawcett, 'A group of churches by the architect of Great Walsingham', to be published in *Norfolk Archaeology*.
32. William, Lord Morley left funds for the nave in 1379 at which time he described it as 'now begun' (Norwich Consistory Court Wills, 160 Heydon).
33. Erwin Panofsky, *Gothic Architecture and Scholasticism*, 1951 (Meridian edn.), 85.
34. Little Cressingham has a wall arcade only in the south aisle, possibly because the north wall may have been retained from an earlier building.
35. The architect of Swanton Morley employed a similar combination of forms in the bases of his nave arcades, except that the bases were less widely projecting.
36. The 14th-century work on the choir and octagon of Ely cathedral has five types of piers and responds, all of which are variants on one theme; however, four show closer kinship with each other in their use of essentially similar base forms, the upper mouldings of which are of very slight projection and are carried on stocks decorated with hollow chamfers like the fluting of

Greek Doric columns. The fifth type of pier, which is employed in the north arcade, has a different base form, and may be the work of a second architect: this change of design may possibly be associated with changes at a higher level in the choir which are seen most clearly in the outer gallery walls and the clerestory.

37. Paul Frankl, *Gothic Architecture* (Harmondsworth 1962), 221–22.
38. Stewart, quoting *Anglia Sacra*, I, 644 and 652.
39. See note 21 above.
40. Reconstructed after the spire collapsed on the choir in the course of a storm of 1361.
41. John Eppe in 1377 made a bequest for furnishings in the chapel of the Holy Trinity on the north side of the church, presumably in the transept (Norwich Consistory Court Wills, 143 Heydon).

Short Contributions

Denny Abbey

By Tony Baggs

The successive ownerships of the monastic site at Denny have been described in print on various occasions — notably in VCH, *Cambridgeshire*, II (1948), pp. 259–62, 295–302 for the documentary background, and in the *Archaeological Journal*, CXXIV, for 1967, pp. 232–34 for the building history. The purpose of this note is to suggest an alternative interpretation of the evidence for the first, Benedictine, phase of occupation which lasted from *c*.1159 to 1170. The surviving structures of that date are the crossing and transepts, up to eaves level, the first pier of the north nave arcade, and the first bay and second pier of the south arcade. Excavations east of the crossing have shown that there was an aisled chancel of at least two bays, and west of the crossing that the footings were laid out for a nave of four bays. The scars of a cut-back half shaft on the north face of the north arcade pier are evidence that a north aisle was intended and this inference is supported by the blocked opening into the north transept. The position of the intended cloister, and hence of the main domestic buildings, is not certain but the north wall of the transepts has an original window at first level and quoins whilst the south wall is later- and post-medieval, suggesting that the south end is the more probable one for extension into an east claustral range. The ground to the south of the church is above the level of the surrounding fen and there is no reason why the usual Benedictine layout should not have been followed. The evidence for a northern cloister relates to the period after the abandonment of the original plan for an aisled nave, and hence to the later Romanesque phase of building associated with the occupation of the Knights Templar.

ACKNOWLEDGEMENTS

I am grateful to Mrs P. M. Christie and to J. G. Coad for allowing me to visit the excavations which they directed at Denny for the Department of the Environment.

Ramsey Abbey

By Tony Baggs

In the *Archaeological Journal*, CXXIV, for 1967 the late P. G. M. Dickinson published a conjectural plan of Ramsey Abbey which was based on the assumption, which had been given substance by the Royal Commission on Historic Monuments, *Huntingdonshire* (1926), that the 13th-century building which forms the south-eastern corner of the later house was the Lady chapel of the abbey and that the east end of the monastic church must therefore have been close to it. Neither the Royal Commission nor Dickinson had noticed that the lower courses of the boundary wall dividing the burial ground of the present parish church from the gardens of the house incorporates lengths of late-medieval walling with an internal offset and the bases of attached shafts. The probable interpretation of these walls is that they are the north and west sides of the north transept of the abbey church. If this is so then the centre of the nave would have been about 300 ft north of the position suggested by Dickinson and the 13th-century building is 250 ft south east of the crossing. In that location it is unlikely that it was part of the abbot's house or the infirmary.

The Restoration of the Lady Chapel Stained Glass

By Dennis King

The conservation of stained glass at Ely cathedral during the last twenty years is not to be compared with Canterbury or York, and is only similar to Norwich by reason of the very scant survival of medieval glass, and the even smaller amount *in situ*, in both cases due to the iconoclasm of the Reformation and the Puritans. At Ely a window was made available (the Will Spens memorial) to receive glass collected and salvaged from various windows during the stonework repairs and other improvements. This presented opportunities for specialised cleaning and preservation techniques on badly corroded glass, and also the challenge of re-creating from these disconnected fragments an aesthetically satisfying east window of a chapel.

We kept back only the 14th-century glass which belonged to the few surviving 'heads' and tracery lights of the famous Lady chapel, also now removed for conservation and possible redeployment after stonework repairs. Work can only proceed slowly until more funds are available, but this will allow more time for conservation problems to be resolved. We found some glass in its original leading but this was too broken and brittle for retention.

Ely, like Norwich and Wells, has benefitted from the importation of glass in the early 19th century, as will be seen in the 16th-century panels from the church of St John the Evangelist, Rouen, now cleaned and releaded into the west window.

Conservation techniques used include ultra-sonic baths and descaling; glass fibre and airbrasive cleaning and a little external Viacryl coating, with and without plating; some very limited resurfacing and repolishing, again with and without sealed plating; edge-joining breaks with silicons (multi-cracked panes plated) or joining, where grazed, with fine leading.

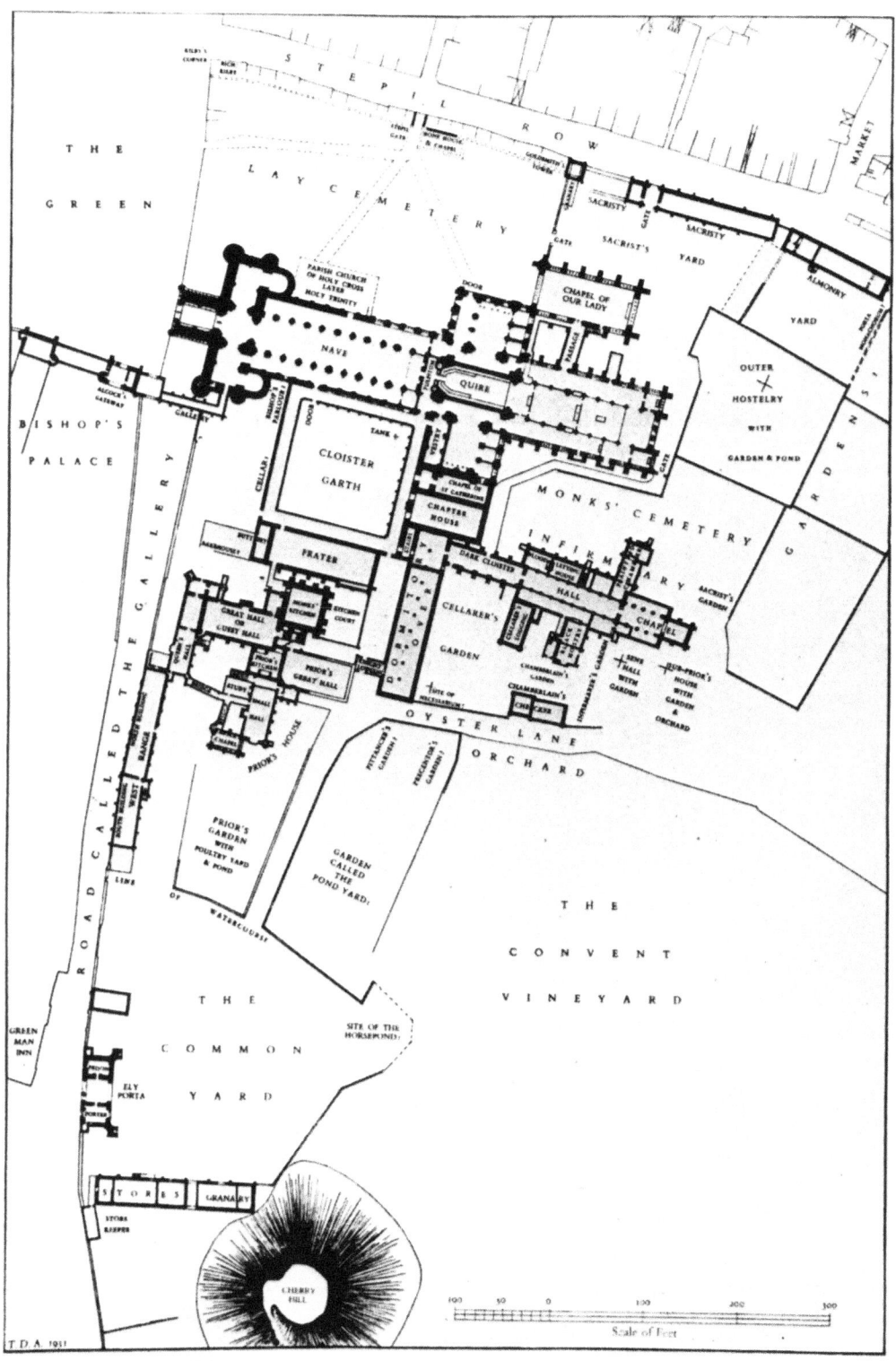

Pl. I. Plan of the monastic precinct *by* T. D. Atkinson

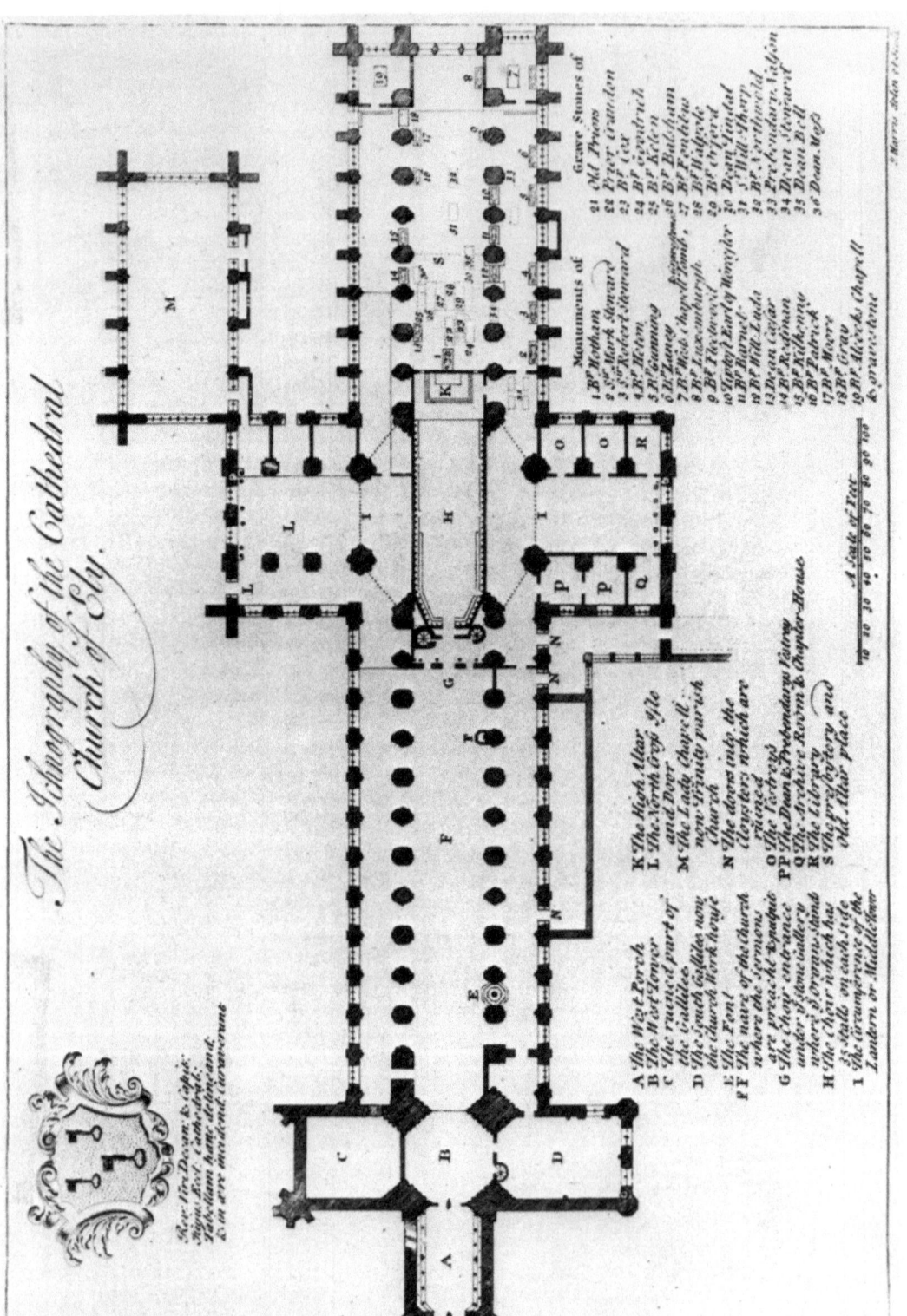

Pl. II. Plan *by* Browne Willis (1742)

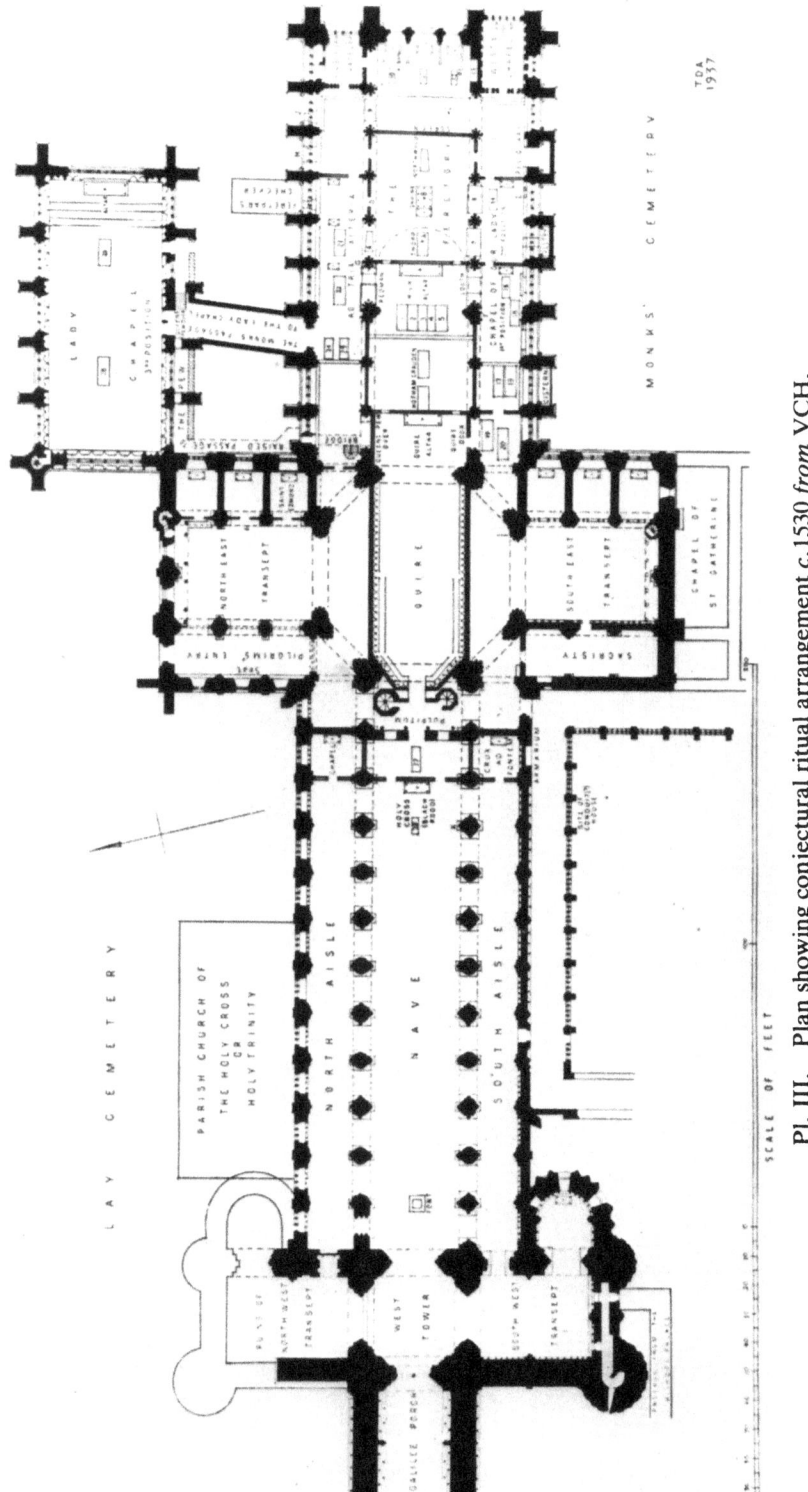

Pl. III. Plan showing conjectural ritual arrangement c.1530 *from* VCH, *Cambridge and the Isle of Ely*, IV (1953)

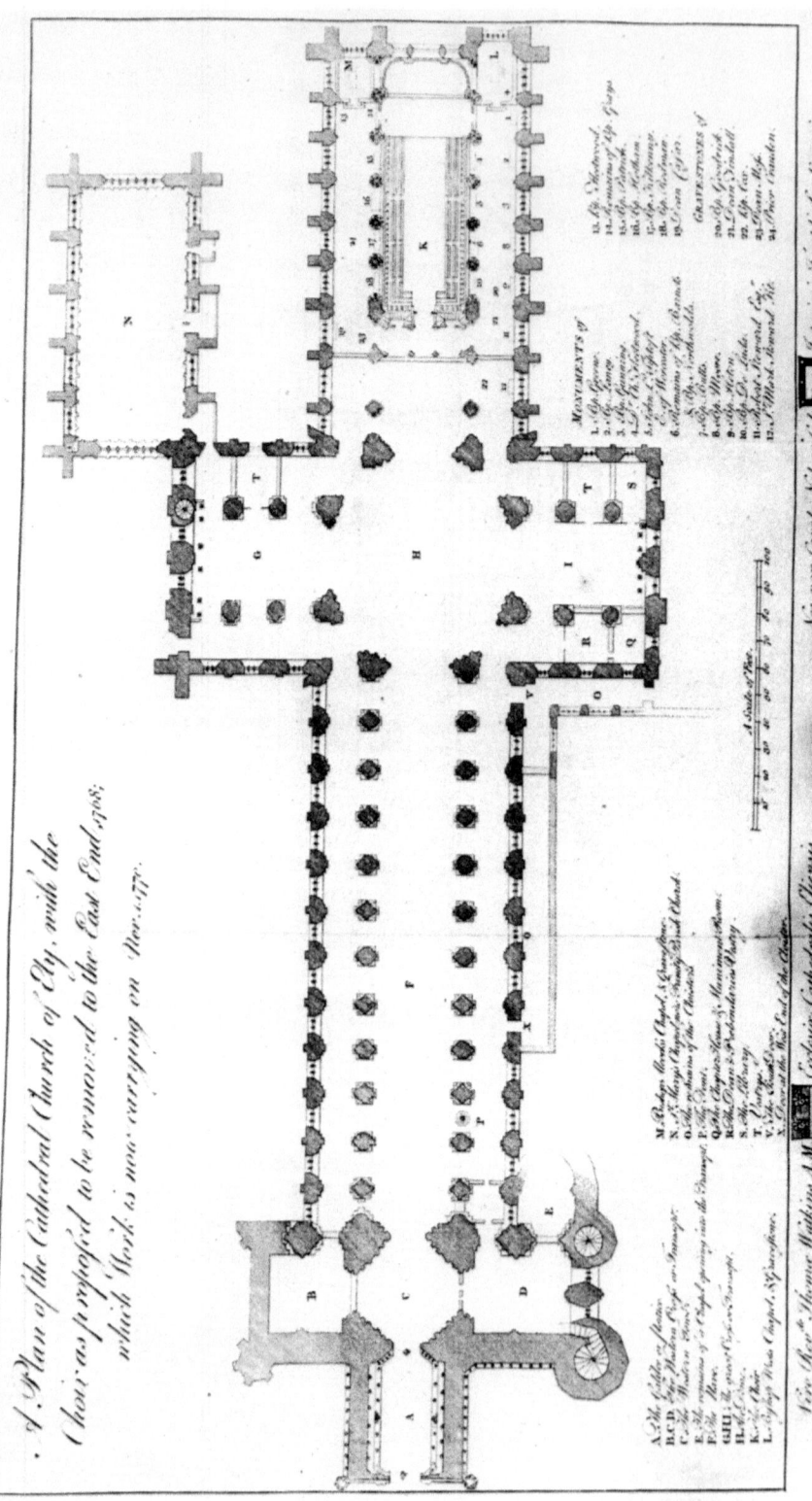

Pl. IV.   Plan showing James Essex's projected alteration to the liturgical arrangement *from* James Bentham

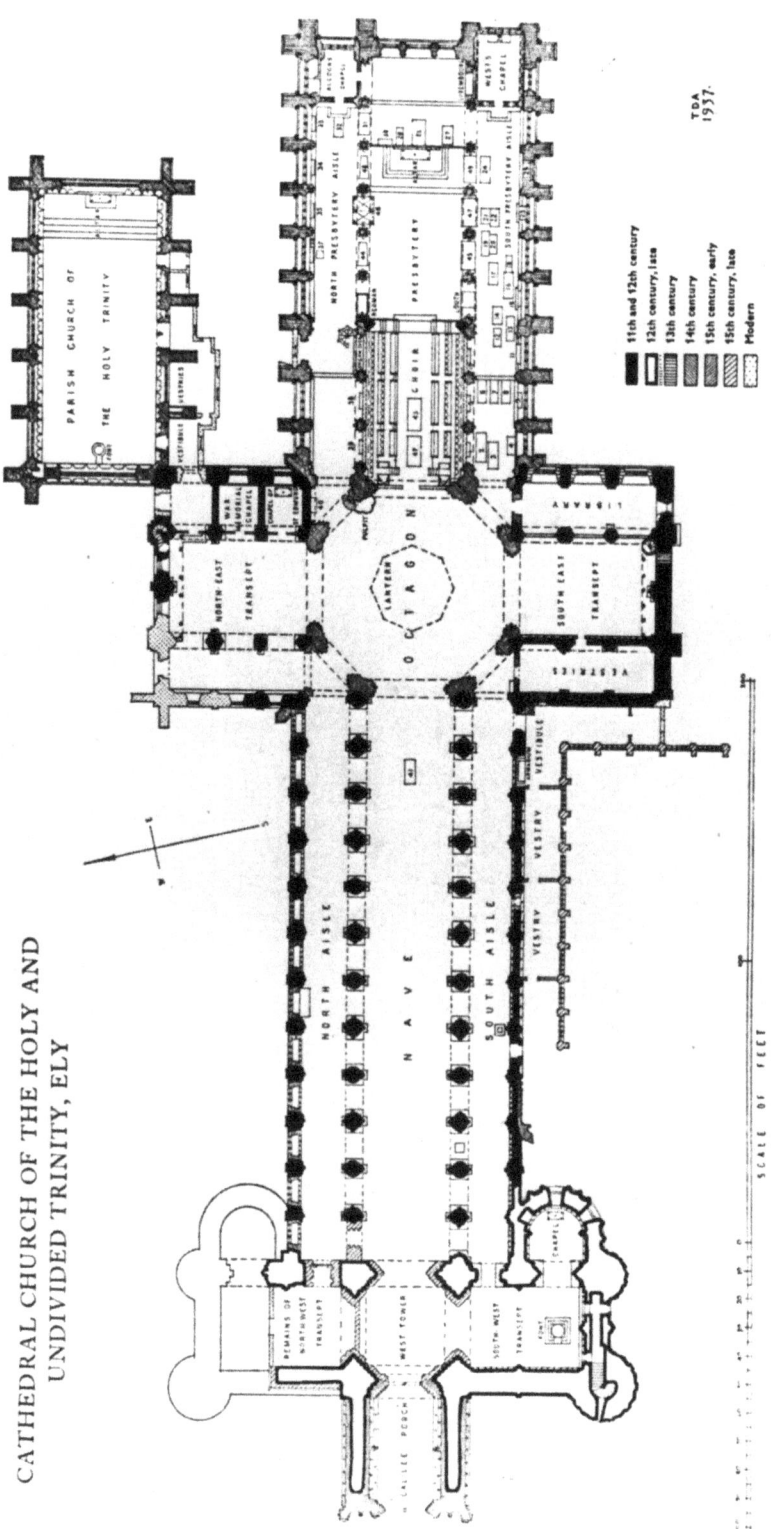

Pl. V. Plan showing present liturgical arrangement as established by G. G. Scott in 1848, from VCH, *Cambridge and the Isle of Ely*, IV (1953)

Pl. VI. Longitudinal section *from* James Bentham

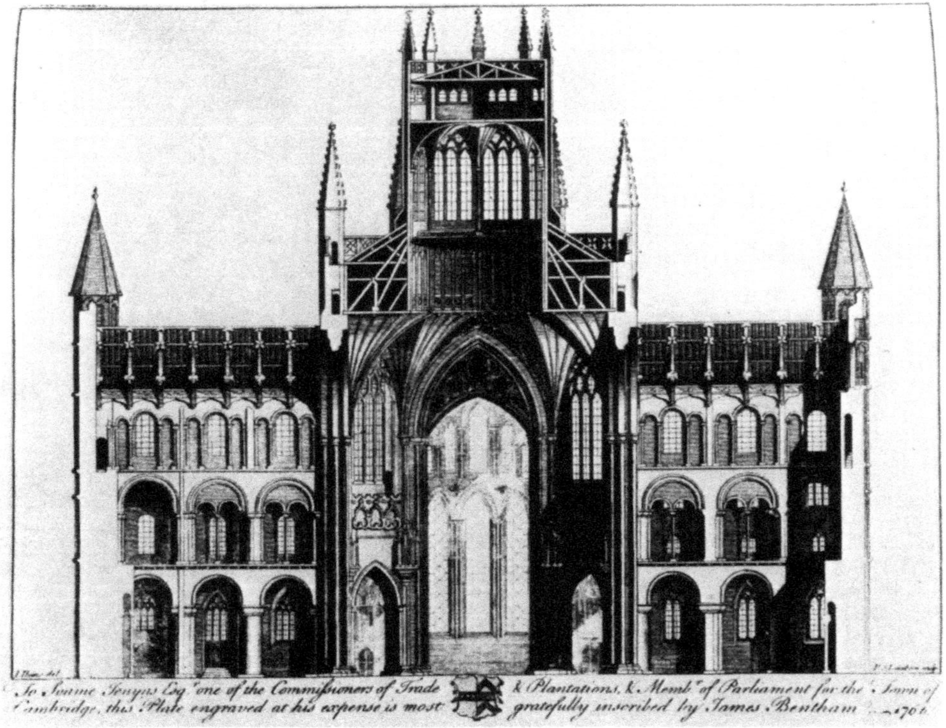

Pl. VIIA. Section through transepts *from* James Bentham

Pl. VIIB. Interior of octagon *from* James Bentham

Pl. VIII.   S elevation of choir

Pl. IX.   N elevation of presbytery

Pl. X. S choir aisle, narrow bay at junction with presbytery aisle (ogee arch and gable restored).
National Monuments Record

Pl. XI. N choir aisle looking W

Pl. XIIA. Prior Crauden's chapel, interior looking E. *National Monuments Record*

Pl. XIIB. Lady chapel, interior, NE corner. *Courtesy Courtauld Institute of Art*

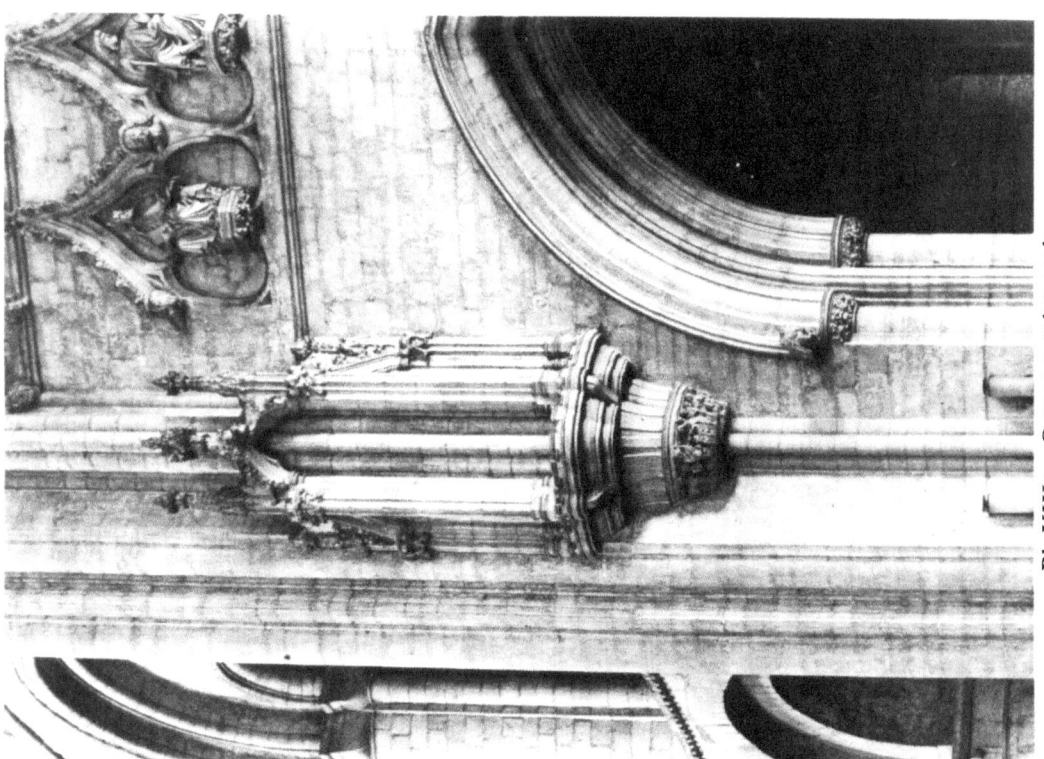

Pl. XIIIA. Octagon, tabernacle.
National Monuments Record

Pl. XIIIB. N choir aisle doorway.
National Monuments Record

Pl. XIVA. Lady chapel, Presentation of the Virgin in the Temple.
Courtesy Courtauld Institute of Art

Pl. XIVB. Lady chapel, Apostles in procession.
Courtesy Courtauld Institute of Art

Pl. XIVc. Octagon, St Etheldreda's staff takes root and blossoms.
Photo F. H. Crossley, © *Canon Ridgway*

Pl. XVA. Lady chapel, wall niches.
Courtesy Courtauld Institute of Art

Pl. XVB. Lady chapel, wall niches

Pl. XVIA. Norwich cathedral: cloister, tracery of S range. *National Monuments Record*

Pl. XVIB. Lady chapel, shaft and base in wall niche. *Courtesy Courtauld Institute of Art*

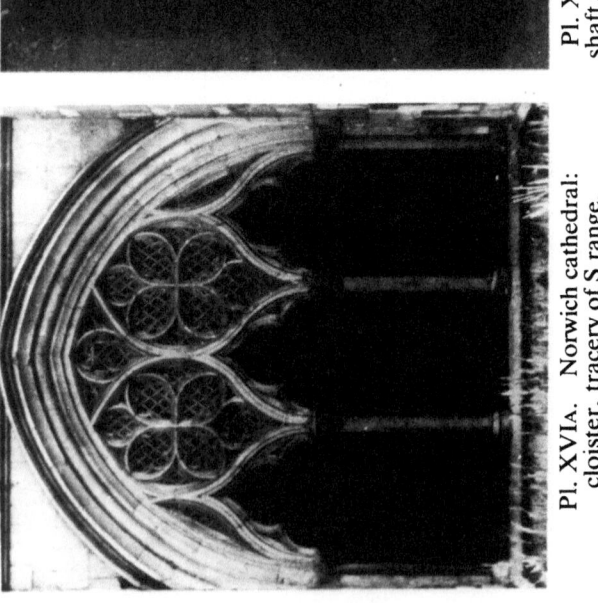

Pl. XVIC. Norwich cathedral: Bishop Salmon's porch. *Photo R. K. Morris*

Pl. XVIF. N transept, NW tourelle

Pl. XVIE. N transept, pinnacle on NW corner

Pl. XVID. N transept, NE tourelle

Pl. XVIIB. Tomb of Bishop Hotham
from James Bentham

Pl. XVIIA. Tomb of Bishop de Luda
from James Bentham

Pl. XVIIIa. N transept, interior, W elevation.
Courtesy Courtauld Institute of Art

Pl. XVIIIb. N transept, exterior.
National Monuments Record

Pl. XIXA. E end in the nineteenth century.
National Monuments Record

Pl. XIXB. S transept, exterior.
National Monuments Record

Pl. XX. Prior Crauden's chapel, plan of tile pavement published 1801 by W. Fowler.
Courtesy Society of Antiquaries of London